Healing of a Wounded Idealist

Healing of a Wounded Idealist

Subject Heading: CHRISTIAN \ CYNICISM\IDEALISM \ FAITH

ISBN: 978-0-620-76831-3

Cover: Sean Kreusch. http://vision-imc.com

To Elena and Luke

Our treasures.
May you always face the future
with courage and kindness.

Contents

Acknowledgments

We have heard it said that writing a book is like having a child. We can heartily attest to the truth of that statement. This book has become our third child. It has demanded our attention, been remarkably needy and won't take no for an answer. We have needed a village to raise this child and thankfully God has surrounded us with people with the willingness and expertise to help us.

Firstly, we want to thank Christian Ray and Deb de Flores for encouraging us to write what God had put on our hearts. We also want to thank Mike and Daphne Renton for patiently enduring our first attempts. Those were some long nights and discussions. Thanks to Roger Dickinson and Bandile Sikwane for your honesty in refining the content, and to Jody De Reuck who kept an eye on it as a psychologist. Thanks also to Gordon Ferguson for his generosity in reviewing it with kindness and insight. Thank you to our brilliant editors, Vida Li Sik, Karen Suchecki and Marc Jarchow. Your diligence has been astounding. We would also like to thank Mike and Anne-Brigitte Taliaferro for a lifetime of friendship and mentoring. You have set examples of what true faith looks like.

But mostly we thank God who has given us our lives and a life together.

Justin and Irene Renton
Johannesburg, South Africa

The Wounded Idealist

*Out of the goodness of your love,
deliver me. For I am poor and needy,
and my heart is wounded within me.*[1]

When I was in my early 20s, a friend quoted an observation of life that went something like this:

*In your 20s you are an idealist, in your 30s
a realist and in your 40s you become a cynic.*

As a fully-fledged idealist and Christian believer, I found it an amusing saying that I never imagined would apply to my life. I regularly repeated it in a half-pitying way as to the fate of the rest of humanity.

Now sitting in my mid-40s, I begrudgingly had to admit that despite my best efforts and optimistic outlook, I had become a cynic. A Christian cynic, but a cynic nonetheless.

I have always hated the word *cynic*. It implies a negative, bitter view of life and relationships. Oscar Wilde

---

[1] Psalm 109:21b- 22

put it like this: "A cynic is a man who knows the price of everything, and the value of nothing."[2] Although I never wanted to be *that* person, life in a broken world had tainted my view and muddied my hope for what the future held. Disappointment can do that to you. It has a way of altering who you are and how you relate to people and to God. The world-renown neurologist and founder of psychoanalysis, Sigmund Freud wrote, "In the depths of my heart, I can't help being convinced that my dear fellow-men, with a few exceptions, are worthless."[3] What a terrible conclusion to come to after years of study and dedication to helping people. And yet, even as a Christian, I felt the trajectory of my own heart leading me down a similar path and conclusion, and it had to stop! But how? There had to be another way – a way in which a person's devotion to God and his purposes was not ravaged by their experience of life on earth.

My husband, in an attempt to steady my faith, introduced me to the concept of a wounded idealist. He had come across it in the book *Faith and Doubt*, by John Ortberg in which he states, "If you scratch under the surface of a cynic you will find a wounded idealist."[4] The

[2] Wilde, O. Lady Windermere's Fan, A Play About a Good Woman. (1892)
[3] Roazen, P. Freud and His Followers. (1992) Da Capo Press
[4] Ortberg, John. Faith and Doubt. (2008) Zondervan

light at the end of the proverbial tunnel switched on.

The notion of being a wounded idealist rather than a hardened cynic resonated with me. It sounded more hopeful. It implied that rather than accept cynicism as a newly cemented temperament, it was a condition that could be healed.

Initially, I attempted to find further Christian literature that addressed the issue of returning to faith from cynicism. While there are many inspirational books out there, I never found anything that fully spoke to what I was going through. In several books, Christian cynicism was discussed as a philosophical ideology (most of it beyond my comprehension), in others, it was alluded to briefly and in still others; it was addressed from an apologetics or Christian evidence standpoint. What I was looking for was a practical guide that would take me step by step back to faith. This was my first problem. My second problem was that being an idealist, I tend to have a short attention span. I need you to dispense with superfluous word buffering and tell it to me straight. This nature has, on my part, resulted in many great spiritual books being either half-read or partially skimmed through. I wanted to find a book, a guide that I could read from cover to cover and it needed to *be short and to the point*. I wasn't looking for a verbal massage, I was looking for help. Having little luck finding such a book, and without knocking what other much more qualified writers had written, my husband and I decided to co-author a book that could be a guide back to faith. It would be honest, vulnerable, practical and direct.

They say that as a writer, when you shape a book, it shapes you. As we have embarked on this endeavor, I have been forever shaped. My cynical heart has already changed form. God is molding something new, and where it ends I am not quite sure but as Carl Sandburg so aptly noted, "I am an idealist. I don't know where I am going, but I am on my way."[5] I have started my journey from wounding to healing and from idealism to faith and hopefully, am able to help a few fellow stragglers or should I say fellow strugglers along the way.

My wife's journey became *our* journey. I am a realist. It may be a combination of a phlegmatic personality and an engineering mind, but life has always been straightforward for me. At the tender age of 10, it became apparent to me that the world was less than ideal and that life was harder than I imagined. I simply readjusted my expectations and moved on. The same is true of my experience in the church. I didn't grow up religious. My

---

[5] Sandberg, C. Incidentals.(1904) Asgard Press

dad was an atheist, my mom an alcoholic.

As remarkable as the church was, it didn't take long for me to realize that it was not a perfect place - not by a long shot. Unlike my wife, that never bothered me. I accepted the reality and moved on. The thought of becoming cynical never appealed to me. If anything, it perplexed me. Why would anyone choose to think so negatively about life, relationships, and even God?

And yet the Bible is peppered with the words of heartbroken cynics.

Consider the following passage of Scripture:

"When your words came, I ate them;
they were my joy and my heart's delight,
for I bear your name, Lord God Almighty.
I never sat in the company of revelers,
never made merry with them;
I sat alone because your hand was on me
and you had filled me with indignation.
Why is my pain unending
and my wound grievous and incurable?
You are to me like a deceptive brook,
like a spring that fails."

"You are to me like a deceptive brook, like a spring that fails." Have more cynical words ever been spoken about God?

And yet these are the words of the great Prophet Jeremiah.[6]

Or how about Job? We know he faced formidable challenges sanctioned by God. The initial dignity and trust with which he faced these trials gave way to bitterness and despair. Cynicism had taken hold of his heart when he complained:

> "Even if I summoned him and he responded,
> *I do not believe* he would give me a hearing.
> He would crush me with a storm
> and multiply my wounds for no reason.
> He would not let me catch my breath
> but would overwhelm me with misery."[7]

I had read these passages before but never understood their implication. As perplexed as I may have been by cynics, God seems unmoved by them. He unabashedly displays their words for all to see. He grants us access into their deepest misery and disillusionment, even their disillusionment with him. He doesn't conceal their disappointment or defend his position.

The Bible is not an idealistic recounting of the history

---

[6] Jeremiah 15:16-18 (emphasis added)
[7] Job 9:16-18 (emphasis added)

of God's people. Through the Scriptures, God introduces us to men and women with whom we can relate. There are flawed heroes, repentant sinners, remorseless villains and wounded idealists, their stories all far from perfect. I recognized that as a leader, husband, father, and friend I needed to learn to better minister to those wounded around me.

As we have written this book, we have been amazed at how differently we see and think about the same situations. We have discussed and debated our own viewpoints and considered each other's. This book is written from both an idealist and realist's perspective and we try to give you an authentic view of both. We start with definitions of all the basic temperaments and focus on the strengths and weaknesses of an idealist. (This would be an equally illuminating exercise to do with realists, but that will have to be for another time.) We speak about what wounds an idealist and why it is an important issue to unpack. From there we take a look at idealists in the Bible and how they found their way to genuine faith, we then take a diversion to examine the insidious nature of self-pity, we go on to challenge a cynic's question and hopefully end at a conclusion that facilitates the formation of faith.

Our goal in all this is that if you or someone you know

has started down the path of cynicism, this book will provide another way. A way in which we are able to find God in the chaos of life, and not be wounded by it.

Why did the Realist, the Idealist and the Cynic cross the road?

Cynicism is dangerous because it turns anger into a virtue.
Andre Maurois

First things first, what is an idealist?

As a point of reference from which to begin, the Merriam-Webster dictionary offers the following definitions for basic human nature.[8]

pes·si·mist

A person inclined to emphasize adverse aspects, conditions, and possibilities. An individual who expects the worst possible outcome.

re·al·ist

A person concerned with fact or reality and rejects the impractical and visionary.

---

[8] Merriam-Webster.com. 2017

ide·al·ist
A person guided by principles or hopes rather than by practicality. Someone who looks on the more favorable side of life and events, expecting the best outcome. Someone who envisions an ideal world rather than reality.

cyn·ic
A person who distrusts other people and believes that everything is done out of self-interest. A person whose outlook is scornfully negative and skeptical.

The familiar phrase "seeing the glass as half empty or half full" describes people's tendency to see the same situation differently.

Take a look at the image below, what do you see?

The pessimist sees the glass as half empty, the idealist as half full, the realist sees a glass with water in it, and the cynic is suspicious as to why it matters.

Definitions Through Examples

This bias to see things differently plays out with remarkable consistency in day-to-day life. For example, let's imagine that a cynic, a pessimist, a realist, and an idealist are invited to interview for the same job.

When the cynic gets the call to come in, he debates whether or not he will go. He doubts that there will be any real chance of him getting the job as the company is more than likely just interviewing a "quota" of external applicants to abide by the law, and will end up hiring internally anyway. He decides to give it a miss.

The pessimist is barely in the building when he notices the receptionist giving him an odd look. He wonders why he applied for the job in the first place and doubts he will get it. He sits in the interview already defeated and interprets the body language of the interviewer as confirmation of his imminent rejection.

The realist arrives at the interview with restrained hope. It is the second interview he has been to in the last month.

The interviewer may or may not like him. He will present his credentials as fairly as possible and hope for the best.

The idealist arrives at the interview convinced that he is the right person for the job and that the job is perfect for him. It is the first interview he has been to. He notices the way the receptionist greets him. He is obviously already a standout. He expects to impress the interviewer and get the job. He has imagined how the interview will play out since the day he got the call to come in. He has envisioned the warmth with which he will be received and the quick-witted answers he will give to the questions asked.

The pessimist, being the most qualified for the position ends up getting the job. He is surprised and expects to be fired within the first six months. The realist, knowing that he can't expect to get every job he interviews for, accepts the reality and moves on to the next interview. The idealist, on the other hand, is shocked that he didn't get the job. He had envisioned the directors marveling at how well he interviewed and at how much they wanted him on board. He spends the next day moping about until he comes across another perfect job, one he is sure to get this time.

Or how about this example: imagine that you threw a party and invited a cynic, a pessimist, a realist and an idealist.

The cynic declines the invitation upfront. She has been to enough parties to know that she doesn't want to attend another one.

The pessimist accepts the invitation with a shrug, mumbling something about a gluten allergy and wondering if you care enough to change the menu. She expects the party to be a disappointment but insists on attending anyway. Once at the party, she will be sure to mention the unfavorable weather conditions, her dislike of football and her irritable bowel. It will be enough to make you wonder why you invited her in the first place!

The realist accepts the invitation with a smile. She won't spend much time thinking about the party. She may even need a reminder of the time and place. She arrives with few expectations and goes with the flow, taking the good and the bad in her stride.

The idealist, however, comes with great expectations. She has already imagined the whole evening in her mind. The anticipation of an event brings her as much, if not more joy than the event itself. She foresees a warm welcome and adequate attention given to her engaging personality.

By the end of the night, the only one walking away potentially disappointed is the idealist. The pessimist assumed it would be a bust, so her expectation was either met or exceeded. The realist never had many expectations, so she enjoyed a night out with friends. But the idealist with her unrealistically high expectations was bound to come back down to earth with the less-than-perfect reception, guest list, and conversation.

Do You See Yourself?

By now, you can probably predict the plot for these examples:

A pessimist, realist, and an idealist book a vacation …
A pessimist, a realist, and an idealist decide to lose weight…
A pessimist, a realist, and an idealist get married…
A pessimist, a realist, and an idealist go into the full-time ministry…
(Not sure of the pessimist going for the last one, but we'll leave it in for consistency's sake.)

These common scenarios play out over and over again, with laughable predictability. And yet for some of us, because of a lack of self-awareness, we aren't able to connect the dots and recognize the patterns. We are convinced that the reason we respond the way we do is because of our boss, our spouse, the minister or the interviewer. What we fail to see is how our interpretation of the situation based on our temperament can affect our reactions.

Self-Awareness is Essential

As Christians, self-awareness is essential for spiritual maturity. The Proverbs teach, "The wisdom of the prudent is to *give thought to their ways*." [9] The older we get, the more conscious we should become of the lenses through which we look at life. These include temperament, culture, upbringing and past experiences (both good and bad).

We cannot underestimate the effect that a *lack* of self-awareness in these areas has on our relationship with God and others. For years I (Irene), could not understand why I saw God as punitive, quick to correct and even quicker to punish. It wasn't until I realized that I had projected the image of my earthly father onto God, assuming they were

---

[9] Proverbs 14:8 (emphasis added)

21

the same. My father was a great dad, but maintaining order in a home with eight children meant that he was quick on the draw when it came to discipline. As a young Christian, I interpreted situations through this "earthly-father" lens. I was sure that God was always angry or disappointed in me. Building intimacy and connection were a struggle, because I was afraid of God but had no idea how to fear him in the biblical sense. Self-awareness was the key that enabled me to correct my distorted view of God. [10]

Interestingly, I also struggled with understanding the fear of God, but for entirely different reasons. While my wife's upbringing was more like the Von Trapp family from *The Sound of Music*, mine was a more casual affair. When I was seven years old, my father told me that he wanted to be my friend and so I should no longer call him dad but rather by his first name, Mike. I know that for some this is heresy! For me, it was how life was. Even from a schooling perspective, things were dramatically different. Every report card for my wife involved detailed interrogation from her father. I, on the other hand, don't ever remember my parents even asking to *see* one of my report cards. They may have, but it was obviously not a memorable event. Needless to say, coming from such

---

[10] For an in-depth study on how our relationship with our physical father can affect our view of God and how to change it, please see Appendix B.

different backgrounds, parenting in the Renton household has been an artful negotiation!

If you are an idealist, you need to gain an awareness of how that nature influences your perspective on life and relationships, how it affects your decision-making and choices, and how it can be potentially harmful.

In reality, most of us start off as idealistic dreamers. As children, life is full of endless possibilities. Young boys dream of becoming firefighters and astronauts, and young girls dream of being fairy princesses and ballerinas.[11] Imagination and fantasy open a world of promise and hope. (We have seen this to be true even of young children living in the direst of circumstances.)

As we age, life in a fallen world has a way of sobering us, thus tempering our imaginations and expectations. We take on a more realistic point of view. But for some, idealistic thinking perpetuates well into early adulthood and beyond. These idealists, of all the temperaments, are

---

[11] A 2015 study by Forbes magazine found that this is no longer true. Most boys now want to become professional athletes or entertainers and most girls want to be doctors. www.forbes.com/sites/.../what-kids-in-2015-want-to-be-when-they-grow-up

the greatest visionaries; and the ones most likely to have their hearts broken.

Strengths of Idealists:

- Idealists are optimistic and bold in their outlook. They face the future and difficulties with hope and high expectations.
- They dream of an ideal world, where things make sense and where everything – good and bad, happens for a reason.
- Idealists want to make the world a better place, so when they find a cause to get behind, they are enthusiastic and energetic. You will find them in churches, charities, non-governmental organizations and the battle rooms of political campaigns. On campus, you are sure to find an idealist sitting behind the sign-up table of any society with the tagline, "SAVE THE …".
- Idealists are dreamers and visionaries, able to "experience" and envision a different reality with incredible clarity.

In his intriguing book, *Stumbling on Happiness*, Harvard psychologist Daniel Gilbert, explains how the brain's frontal lobe enables us to envision the future. He writes, "The greatest achievement of the human brain is its ability to imagine objects and episodes that do not exist in the realm of the real." It was this ability that made it possible for man to advance and move from the savannahs and jungles to the cities we live in today. It is this vision that gave birth to the Seven Wonders of the Ancient World and the marvel of space exploration. "The idealists and visionaries, foolish enough to throw caution to the winds and express their ardor and faith in some supreme deed, have advanced mankind and have enriched the world."[12] And advance mankind they have.

If you are an idealist, you may be feeling rather good about yourself. Here's where a full understanding of the temperament God has given you comes into play. Gilbert goes on to say, "We cannot do without reality and we cannot do without illusion. Each serves a purpose, each imposes a limit on the influence of the other, and our experience of the world is the artful compromise that these tough competitors negotiate." [13] We need illusion, and vision but we also need *reality*.

This brings us to the weaknesses of idealists.

---

[12] Goldman, E. Anarchism and other essays. (1910) Mother Earth Publishers
[13] Gilbert, D. T. Stumbling on happiness. (2007) Knopf

Weaknesses of Idealists:

- Idealists tend to be inexperienced and naïve.
- They are easily disappointed and surprised when the results they hoped for do not materialize.
- The concept of "you reap what you sow" is lost to young idealists. They tend to be big dreamers and talkers, and not necessarily big doers. They fail to realize the amount of hard work, patience, and endurance it will take to reach their goals or bring about the change they desire.
- When describing situations, idealists can exaggerate the good and ignore the facts. (If we go back to the interview, the idealist would have explained how well he was received. The fact that he was under-qualified for the job would have, in his mind, been irrelevant.)
- Measuring life by their idealistic yardstick they can have unrealistic expectations of God, themselves and others. Consequently, they can be critical of people who do not see life as they do.
- Grey areas, disputable matters, and fuzzy boundaries can be quite unsettling for idealists. They tend to think in black and white, a thing is either right or wrong. While having strong convictions, they can lack mercy in dealing with other people.

- Suffering is also a difficult notion for idealists to wrap their heads around. It confuses them. They have difficulty accepting or dealing with their own suffering, real and imagined, as well as others. They are eager to find ways to reduce or alleviate it.

- Idealists tend to be impatient. When an idealist prays for something, they expect it to happen ... now. They consider the fact that they prayed believing entitles them to a quick response from their heavenly Father. While God may work miraculously in circumstances, many times he will allow the natural processes or laws of life to take place. This can be a source of great frustration and discouragement for an idealist. An idealist needs to embrace the concept that SO MUCH OF FAITH IS PATIENCE!

- They can also give into regular bouts of self-pity.

When we become Christians, we bring with us the strengths and weaknesses of our God-given temperaments. Despite what some may think, at baptism, our sins get washed away, we don't get a personality transplant.

If you are an idealist, wounded or otherwise, you need to become cognizant of the influence idealistic thinking has on the initial excitement to follow Christ, your ability to handle disappointments and the potential for disillusionment. If an idealist does not reset their lenses and change their frame of reference, then as the proverbs say, hope deferred *will make* the heart sick.[14]

Our goal is that the next chapters will enable you to change the faulty lenses and references that have guided your perspective. Armed with the faith that God heals the brokenhearted and binds up their wounds, let the healing begin!

---

[14] Proverbs 13:12

What Wounds an
Idealist?

*An idealist is one who, on noticing
that roses smell better than
cabbage, concludes that it will
also make better soup.*
HL Mencken

A while ago, I was asked to share the opening class for
women who serve in the full-time ministry in the
International Churches of Christ. Around 18 000
Christians from all over the world were to gather in St
Louis, Missouri, to be inspired and encouraged in their
faith. I was to be one of those encouragers.

I gladly accepted the honor of speaking at such an
event, hoping to get an opportunity to speak on prayer or
vulnerability. But instead I was given the title "To the ends
of the earth", with the following tagline:

"This session will feature those amongst us who
maintain the cutting edge of reaching out with faith and
zeal even in the most challenging situations. The class will
provide an opportunity to sit at the feet of some of the

most radical disciples who have devoted their lives to reaching out to save the lost. Look forward to a unique and inspiring presentation of faith and zeal to make disciples of all nations."

I wish I could say I was happy to speak on the topic, but that would be lying. The presentation may well be unique, but I doubted that it would be particularly inspiring. And not for the reasons you would imagine.

A Glimpse into South Africa's History

In 24 years of ministry, I had seen some unbelievable things. I became a Christian in 1989 as an American student living in South Africa, a country still in the grip of apartheid. Nelson Mandela was in prison and would remain there for another 12 months. Decades of segregation had torn society apart. The pass laws, which prohibited the free movement of black South Africans within their own country, were still enforced by law, imprisonment and beatings. South Africa was being heavily sanctioned by nations around the world, and anti-apartheid activism within and outside her borders was reaching a crescendo. The country felt like it was on the cusp of a hopeful future or the threat of collapse into chaos.

In it all, the church stood as a beacon of light. It was the one place where you didn't pay lip service to love across racial lines, but where you were able lay down old prejudices and become family. It intrigued and inspired me. It gave me a vision and purpose for which to spend myself.

Since those days, I have been privileged to be a part of South Africa's history. I was there the day Nelson Mandela was released from prison and addressed the nation in the Cape Town city square. In 1994, I watched the endless queues of people line up to vote in the first democratically held election. The miraculous peace and goodwill that kept the country together during those times were not of this earth. I witnessed the birth of a fledgling democracy and have experienced its growing pains these past 23 years.

In the church, I have seen the gospel spread throughout what was once called the "dark continent." I have witnessed lives changed and marriages healed. I have seen churches planted, locals raised up, and evangelists appointed. I have seen many die faithful and win the ultimate victory.

Why Am I Reluctant?

So, with everything I have seen and experienced, why would I be so reticent to talk about going, "To the ends of the earth?" Why so reluctant to speak about completing the mission that God has left for us? A younger me would have been the first to put up my hand and repeat the words of Isaiah; "Here am I. Send me!"[15] But 27 years into my spiritual journey, my heart was saying, *I am here, send someone else!*

Something was not right. Indeed, it was very wrong. Had I become hard-hearted and stubborn despite my daily devotion to God? Was I comfortable and lazy? Had I become religious? As a women's ministry leader, I had challenged other floundering Christians using these parameters. And yet now, as I sat with the dread of being inauthentic in a speaking assignment, I was lost to what the real problem was. I just felt cynical about it all. Jaded.

When I made the connection between a cynic and a wounded idealist, I recognized that I was wounded.

---

[15] Isaiah 6:8

So What Wounds an Idealist?

Initially, nothing wounds an idealist. That's the nature of idealism. But once an idealist is wounded, everything and anything can be wounding, from unanswered prayers to unnerving political outcomes. In fact, life can be pretty painful as a wounded idealist. You have such high hopes for life and people, little of which manages to match up to your expectations. At the risk of sounding dramatic, I felt like I lived with a low-grade sense of disappointment most of the time.

Of all the things that wound an idealist, nothing is as wounding as relational conflict and disconnect. It can be devastating, a source of disillusionment and despair. In two and a half decades, I had had my fair share of relational disappointments.

I had shared the gospel with many people in the hope of helping them to know God and many had disregarded it. *That hurt.*

I had had Christian friends who I loved and shared my life with deciding to no longer keep the faith. *That burned.*

I had seen spiritual heroes fall, marriages fail, friendships strained, righteousness not upheld, churches divided and prayers unanswered. I had seen one of the most wounding of all, children choosing either not to follow Christ or to turn away from their devotion to Him. *That ached.*

If you are a realist, I hear what you may be saying to yourself. "Come on Irene, these things happen. It's no different to the first-century church. If you look at the New Testament, the early church was fraught with difficulty. In fact, we are yet to hear of a modern church where the members are getting drunk on communion wine or getting involved in indecencies with step-relations, as it describes in the book of 1 Corinthians. We can't possibly think we are above the church led by the apostles."
And you would be right to think and say such things.

It Won't Happen To Me!

But here's the thing you need to understand about an idealist. One of the guiding beliefs that an idealist lives with is that "it will never happen to me (or us)." So while it may have occurred in the first century, surely we, in the 21st century, with all our technology and ability to communicate across the continents, will overcome the problems they had. We can be better; we can be different.

This thinking is not limited to the church. Idealists apply the "it won't happen to me," mentality to most things. They may not verbalize it, but in their hearts; this is their truth. "I won't fail, I won't have difficulty getting an education or finding a job. I won't remain single; I won't have trouble in my marriage or get divorced. I won't remain childless; I won't have complicated pregnancies (or childbirths or children). I won't ..." you can complete the sentence.

It doesn't matter what others have to say on these topics, for an idealist, it won't happen to them, it will be different. The problem comes when it isn't different, when it does happen to them. This comes as a big surprise to the idealist, and the wounding begins.

Possibly one the least liked or least *believed* verses in the Bible for an idealist is where Jesus says, "In this world, you *will* have trouble."[16] I had always read this verse to mean, "In this world, you will have trouble, but not *trouble*, trouble." Not real trouble. Just the sort of trouble that makes you pray more. Certainly not the kind of trouble that forces you to question your faith and trust in God. Not the kind of distress that takes you to the edge of all that you hold dear and requires a re-evaluation. Or the excruciating pain of loss that makes you doubt the very nature of God. No! It will be *insignificant* trouble. The

---

[16] John 16:33 (emphasis added)

kind where you can't find your car keys so you'll be late for a meeting, or where you get a head cold just before an exam. Those kinds of troubles.

Little did I know how unafraid and trusting of us God is, to allow us to go through suffering, to be refined and if needed, even wounded.

An Unexpected Response

Going back to my speaking assignment, as much as I wanted to stand before the leaders with pom-poms and a motivational war cry, I just couldn't bear to do it. I decided to rather share with them what I have shared with you in the hopes of finding my own healing in the process. I was so surprised by the reaction. The response was overwhelming.

The message seemed to hit a collective nerve:

"So thankful that someone is talking about this so openly."
"I want to be faithful but I have been hurt."
"I have become tired of pretending."
"This is so refreshing."
"I see the hurts of people around me and haven't been able to know how to help. This will be a great tool."

"My husband is such an idealist; he needs to hear this!"

Contrary to my idealistic notion, what I was feeling was not unique. People from every walk of life shared with me in person or by email how much they related to what I shared. We shared a common sort of grief, a grief of a dream that was dying. Our hearts were breaking, and we needed another way! It struck me that this was not simply another 'class to teach' but for many, especially older Christians, a critical need.

I was equally amazed at the response of people to Irene's message. There were a lot more wounded idealists out there than I imagined, a whole segment of the church that I had no idea was struggling with these issues. While realists approach life with measured expectations, idealists approach *each day* with high expectations. This is an important difference to be aware of, as John Maxwell points out,

"Disappointment is the gap that exists between **expectation** and **reality**."[17]

------

[17] Maxwell, J. Life Wisdom: Quotes from John Maxwell: Insights on Leadership. (2014) B&H Books

The bigger the gap, the greater the disappointment, and the greater the disappointment the more tentative one becomes in life. When you have been deeply disappointed it's easy to start living in "self-preservation" mode where the end goal is to survive the day, the week, the month or the year. Trying to protect yourself from further hurts stops you from truly living and entrusting your heart to people around you, even the people you really care about. *This is a tragedy.*

Mark Twain observed: "We should be careful to get out of an experience only the wisdom that is in it and stop there; lest we be like the cat that sits down on a hot stove lid. She will never sit down on a hot stove lid again and that is well. But she will never sit down on a cold lid anymore."[18]

Wounded idealists have sat on enough hot stove lids to prevent them from taking a chance with a cold stove lid. They may have expected that once they become Christians, they are guaranteed a rosy life, a fairy tale where... *we all live happily ever after.* Although they may never say it out loud, their bewilderment at suffering and difficulty reflects this belief and expectation. They can look to the church to fix their lives, their families, their

---

[18] Twain, M. Following the Equator. (1987) Sun-Times Media Group

spouses and their children. And because the church is made up of other sinful people it can end up becoming another source of disappointment, discouragement, disillusionment and eventually the bitterness described in Hebrews 12. It is this bitterness that we encounter in cynics, and it is this bitterness that can unsettle realists.

Helping the Wounded Heal

As strange as it may sound, what we have come to realize is that what Christian cynics need most is *compassion*. I know; we were just as surprised! It can be challenging to look past their condescending smirks and at times harsh remarks.

"Yeah right!
Seeing is believing.
Been there, done that.
I don't trust anyone anymore.
What do you really want from me?"

It has been said that giving someone your attention is one of the rarest forms of generosity, and while it may be tempting to retort with sarcasm or irritation; cynics actually need someone to take a moment and see things from their perspective. They need somebody willing to hear their disappointment and disillusionment and to ask "What were you hoping for... what were you expecting?"

Don't discount the cynics around you. Engage with them. If you will engage a wounded idealist and help them to heal, they can become a force for change. Gifted with natural vision and equipped with newfound empathy, they can, we believe, still have great impact on the world around them.

A Case Study: Elijah

*If you expect the world to be fair to you because
you are fair; you are fooling yourself.
That's like expecting the lion not to
eat you because you didn't eat him.*

Anonymous

The Bible's honest recounting of Elijah's life makes him an ideal case study of a wounded idealist who found his way back to faith. Although not a whole lot is written about his life, God chose Elijah as one of the men to encourage Jesus on the Mount of Transfiguration before his suffering and death on the cross.

We read the account of Elijah's faith journey in 1 Kings 17 to 19. He seems to appear out of nowhere and confronts King Ahab whom the Bible describes as doing "more to arouse the Lord's anger than all the kings of Israel before him."[19] He was a wicked, dangerous man but Elijah doesn't flinch; he is bold and confident.

---

[19] 1 Kings 16:33

Enjoying the Mountain Tops

After delivering the message of impending drought, Elijah goes into hiding by a stream where he is miraculously fed by ravens day and night. In time the stream dries up and he becomes the houseguest of a poor widow from Zarephath. God supernaturally provides them with bottomless flour and oil. In time, the widow's son dies, and although there was no biblical record of anyone raising the dead before, Elijah fearlessly prays, and the boy comes back to life. The mission from God was going well for Elijah, and it just kept getting better.

After three years, God tells Elijah to meet up with Ahab again. On the way, he meets Obadiah who tells him that Elijah is not the only prophet left in Israel, but that he had saved 100 others from Ahab's tyranny.[20] Elijah confronts Ahab and summons him to what could best be described as a modern-day face-off. He rounds up the prophets of Baal on Mount Carmel and challenges them to a contest. Despite their enthusiastic efforts, the prophets of Baal failed to "awaken" or "get the attention" of their god, to the great amusement of Elijah who lavishly taunts them from the sidelines. When the time comes for Elijah to represent God, he does so with great bravado and

---

[20] 1 Kings 18:13

42

theatrics. God, in his mercy, humors Elijah, sending fire from heaven, which burned up the sacrifice and everything around it.[21]

When the people see this, they are terrified and acknowledge God as the true God of Israel. Elijah orders them to kill the prophets of Baal and then prays for rain to end the drought. And once again God answers.

What a victory! What a triumph of good over evil! So far everything has gone well for Elijah. He has experienced success after success. He has lived by a stream in a devastating drought, raised the dead, confronted the wicked and wiped out false prophets. The ministry is everything he could have asked for and more. He has been zealous and optimistic with extraordinary results. Optimism, however, only becomes faith *once it is tested*, and Elijah's faith was about to be tested.

Fleeing to the Valleys

After his great victory on Mount Carmel, we read of Ahab's wife's fury at the death of her prophets.[22] She threatens Elijah with the same fate and, terrified, he runs

---

[21] 1 Kings 18:38
[22] 1 Kings 19:2

43

for his life. He runs to the wilderness, to the safety of what he had known for the past three years. Once there, he sits down under a broom tree and prays that he might die. "I have had enough Lord, take my life, I am no better than my ancestors."[23]

Let's take a step back here.
"I have had enough Lord."
He has had enough.
Enough?
Enough of what?
What exactly had he done?

Everything had gone so well for him up until this point. The first serious threat to his faith and Elijah completely unravels. Why would he possibly react this way?

If Elijah had been a pessimist, he might have said: "I knew this wasn't going to work out. I knew Jezebel was going to get upset. Yes, things were going well, but I knew bad times were around the corner, they always are."

If Elijah had been a realist, he may have said something like: "Well it was to be expected. You can't predict the outcome of these things; I need to change my strategy.

---

[23] 1 Kings 19:4

44

Rome wasn't built in a day." But we believe that Elijah was wired as an idealist and for an idealist, when God is on your side, what could go wrong? He is devastated and disillusioned.

In chapter one we looked at a few characteristics of an idealist summarized in the following chart:

Positive traits	Negative traits
Optimistic	Naïve and inexperienced
Wishful thinker	Easily discouraged
Zealous	Confused by suffering
High expectations	Critical of others
Self-sufficient	Lazy
Hopeful	Impractical, rash
Enthusiastic	Wounded by conflict
Bold and willing to try new things	Unrealistic expectation of self and others
Can exaggerate the good and ignore the facts	Given to self-pity

Idealism's Expectations Dashed

In many ways, these characteristics describe Elijah. Let's take a closer look.

First, *he exaggerates the good and ignores the facts.* Earlier we noted that on his way to meet Ahab, Elijah met up with Obadiah who told him that he had saved 100 prophets. Yet shortly after this, in the middle of the face-off, Elijah declares, "I am the only one of the Lord's prophets left."[24]

What a dramatic statement! It was a false statement, but it certainly made for good showmanship. He was aware of at least 100 other prophets and yet he claims to be the only one left. It was the world Elijah had created; it was him and God against the world. He exaggerated the good and ignored the facts.

What about his naivety and unrealistic expectations? Elijah had all the prophets of Baal killed within the borders of two of the most wicked rulers recorded in the Bible. What did he expect would happen next? Possibly, idealistically, that after the great victory, everyone would go home and repent of their sin and idol worship? Maybe

---

[24] 1 Kings 18:22 (emphasis added)

he expected that Ahab would tell Jezebel everything that happened and that she too would repent. And they would all live happily ever after with Elijah as the conquering hero.

But this is not what happens. Instead, Elijah becomes a fugitive, with a "wanted: dead or alive" bounty on his head. He is surprised, confused and deeply disappointed. Our idealistic Elijah has been wounded. He had gotten out of touch with the real world, and it was a rude awakening. He underestimated Jezebel, and it exposed his naivety and inexperience in dealing with evil people. He was visibly shaken by the reality of how difficult God's mission and life could be. Life was no longer exciting. Not everyone repented or was impressed by him or what he stood for. God had become unpredictable; and was no longer a safe place or secure haven for Elijah.

Here's a Scary Thought

We live in South Africa. It is an astoundingly beautiful country with remarkable people, but it still carries the scars of a dysfunctional past. According to global statistics, it is ranked as one of the most dangerous countries to live in, with the 8th highest murder rate in the world.[25] We have experienced crime first-hand. Friends and church members have been hijacked, tied up, beaten up and assaulted. My father and I (Justin) were robbed at home with guns to our heads. Now, while South Africa may not be the safest place to live, nothing on earth can be more frightening than feeling that God doesn't have your back. That he won't be there when you most need him. *That's truly scary!*

And yet, nowhere in the Bible does it say that life *with God* is going to be easy or without its challenges. Nowhere does it say that going through hard times equates to God no longer being with you or protecting you or caring for you.

Finding God in The Wilderness

This is a hard concept for idealists to understand. It was hard for Elijah to understand, so, with a well-rehearsed speech in hand; Elijah goes to meet with God.

> "I have been very zealous for the Lord God Almighty. The Israelites have rejected your covenant, broken down your altars and put to death

[25] https://businesstech.co.za/**south-africa**-is-one-of-the-most-violent-and-unsafe-countries

your prophets with the sword. I am the only one left, and now they are trying to kill me too."[26]

It is less of a meeting and more of a confrontation. Elijah tells God what God already knew. God responds by allowing Elijah to experience his presence, first, in a powerful wind, then in an earthquake, and then a fire. Finally, God appears with a gentle whisper. You would think that Elijah would have gotten the message that God was saying, "It's going to be Ok, Elijah, and despite how it looks I am still in control."

But in his disillusionment, Elijah cannot hear God anymore. He can only see his own pain and responds four verses later by repeating the *exact* same statement he had made earlier.

"I have been very zealous for the Lord God Almighty. The Israelites have rejected your covenant, broken down your altars and put to death your prophets to death with the sword. *I am the only one left* and now they are trying to kill me too."[27]

---

[26] 1 Kings 19:10
[27] 1 Kings 19:14 (emphasis added)

If God had left Elijah in this state, this would have become his defining life statement; the reason for his disillusionment. He would repeat it to friends, family and anyone else who would bother to hear his complaint. And it was a lie.

In front of the prophets of Baal he had boasted that he was the only one of the Lord's prophets left, but now before God, he states it like it is the truth. *A lie had become his truth.* He is negative and bitter and feels justified in his self-pity. He has traded his idealism in for cynicism. It is not a pretty picture, and yet, can't we be the same way? Cynical, jaded, negative and feel justified to be this way.

What is Recorded in Your Heart?

Most people don't set out to be Christian cynics, but like Elijah we can start cementing cynical statements and reasoning in our hearts.

"Well, I used to be very zealous back in the day and even went on a mission team, but I was hurt by this person or that group so now…

I was,
I used to be,

I once, but now…"

What is recorded in your heart?

"I have had good friends turn their backs on God so now…
I had trouble in my marriage so now…
I messed up spiritually so now…
I have seen spiritual heroes fall so now…
I have suffered in relationships so now…
I struggled financially despite trusting God so now…
I was treated harshly by a leader so now …
I didn't know what I was doing and failed so now…
I realize that I am not as talented as others so now…
Someone didn't believe in me so now…
I became chronically ill so now…
God never answered my prayer for a spouse or child so now…
Someone close to me passed away unexpectedly so now…"

The list is endless.
You know your own wounding.

The great news is that Elijah's story didn't end there. God listened to his complaint and then showed him the reality of his situation. Things were not what they seemed. The truth was, despite how Elijah felt, he was not alone. Not only were there 100 prophets left, a further 7 000 in Israel had not bowed to Baal.

Faithful Realism the Goal

As we close this chapter, we want you to consider two things. Firstly, consider how you may have been idealistic in your thinking about God, life, people, the church, and yourself.

- Question whether part of your wounding came from unrealistic expectations from yourself or others.
- What were the unrealistic expectations?
- Take these wounds to God without blaming him, yourself or others. Speak through each one with him and pray that he will show you a different perspective on each situation.

Secondly, if you have been hurt in relationships, forgive. Truthfully, even with the incredible example of forgiveness God has given us in Jesus, forgiveness is a lot harder than we imagine. To quote the famous words of Alexander Pope; "To err is human, to forgive, divine."[28] We need divine intervention!

Idealists can think that because Jesus prayed for unity in John 17, it should come naturally for us to all get along. In reality, relationships take tremendous effort. Don't let that surprise or discourage you. Relationships are a great blessing in this life, but they are also a messy business. Thankfully, God willingly forgives us and enables us to forgive others.

If you are in contact with the person you are struggling to forgive and have a strained relationship, the following may be helpful.

- Pray that the person will forgive you for any hurts that you may have caused them, real or imagined.
- There are times where reconciliation is not possible. **That's ok**. The Bible teaches that, "*If it is possible*, as far as it depends on you, live at peace with everyone."[29] There is an assumption that there may be times where try as you may, reconciliation

---

[28] Pope Alexander, An Essay on Criticism (1711)
[29] Romans 12:18 (emphasis added)

is not possible. What is needed is time and space. Surrender the relationship to God and let him mend it at the right time. You can continue to obey Jesus' command to pray for your enemies.[30] This is not easy, especially when you just want to fix things. But there are times when you just have to let it go.

- *Exquisite Agony (Crucified by Christians)*[31] by Gene Edwards is a tremendous resource in helping individuals to deal with hurts caused by other Christians. We highly recommend it.

When we have been hurt it is hard to think of either taking any responsibility for the hurt or of thinking of forgiving the offending person. God understands. He is a kind and compassionate God. Take your wounded heart to him.

Our Best Days Lie Ahead

It has been said that:
Wisdom is nothing more than healed pain.

Our stories don't have to end at the wounding, the

---

[30] Matthew 5:44

[31] Edwards Gene, Exquisite Agony. (1995). Seedsowers

wounding can be the beginning of wisdom. Elijah went back to the wilderness to seek answers. He found God there. It sometimes takes us going through the wilderness to find God. Elijah's best days came *after* the wounding.

He moved from being a bold idealist to what could best be described as a faithful realist. He became a man able to face facts with faith. He kept his confidence, but now it was placed in God and not in an outcome. He learned to trust that God works in and through difficulties. Elijah gives us an example of a man who not only conquered his outer adversaries but more importantly conquered his inner adversary of flawed reasoning.

A Word on Self-Pity

I never saw a wild thing sorry for itself.
A small bird will drop frozen dead from a bough
without ever having felt sorry for itself.

D.H. Lawrence

Can I Be Really Honest?

Besides my idealistic nature, I have struggled with low-grade depression, or dysthymia, for most of my life. As a women's ministry leader, I am always on the lookout for new ways to deal with it and in turn help others.

Before we embark on this chapter, it is important to note that there are many forms of depression. Scientists believe that its cause can be biological (changes in brain chemistry or genetic pre-disposition), cognitive (the way a person thinks) and sociocultural (stressful life circumstances).[32] There are no quick-fixes or cure-alls to overcoming depression, but as a Christian, several things can be helpful: having someone mature to talk to, learning to trust and obey God in suffering, finding meaning and purpose, and if necessary, seeking professional help which may include taking medication.

---

[32] NIMH. Causes of Depression.*nimh.nih.gov 2011*

What I would like to address in this chapter is the role that self-pity plays in dysthymia. We seldom hear of self-pity spoken about in sermons or Christian literature, but believe that its power to influence our moods and connection to God is gravely underestimated. Our hope is that what is shared can serve to bring some self-awareness and provide an additional tool towards spiritual healing.

Dysthymia is exhausting. Christian psychologists Shapiro and Shapiro describe it as "characterized by a depressed mood for the majority of days over a period of at least two years which includes fatigue, loss of energy, diminished self-esteem, disrupted appetite, impaired concentration and feelings of hopelessness... However, these symptoms are not of such severity as to interfere substantially with family, social, educational or occupational functioning"[33] They go on to say, "We have often surmised that dysthymia is one of Satan's preferred tools for gradually wearing down the resistance of a Christian's soul. Since it does not involve the catastrophic incapacitating experiences that characterize major depression, it is stealthy and insidious."[34]

---

[33] See DSM - 1V description for a fuller explanation

[34] Shapiro and Shapiro, Rejoice Always. (2000) Discipleship Publications International

I can best describe my dysthymia like pushing a shopping cart with a broken wheel around a store. While you can get up and down the aisles, it takes at least double the effort. With dysthymia, while you can function in everyday life, it takes a tremendous effort to mentally and emotionally be involved in even the simplest activities. I experienced times of sadness that felt like the lights in my head had been switched off. It was a tangible darkness, a gloom that made getting out of bed in the morning difficult. Sometimes I felt hopeless. The things that usually excited me no longer gave me joy. At times I wanted to sleep all day, other times I could not sleep at all. Either way, during those times, I wanted to get off the endless merry-go-round of life.

Where Did This Come From?

The worst part for me was that there was seldom any real reason for the way I felt. The depression seemed to come and go without me being aware of what had triggered or lifted it. I felt ashamed at there being no apparent cause. I had every reason to be joyful instead of sad and tired of life. I was afraid to talk about how I felt; it seemed ridiculous. I was sure that no one would understand. I didn't even understand it, how would anyone else?

I tried various supplementary medications with mixed results. I tried to be "more spiritual," thinking that if I read my Bible more or prayed longer, the depression would lift. What I came to find was that while praying and reading are a lifeline, no amount of spiritualizing depression helps unless you identify and deal with the underlying cause or causes.

At times, I accepted it as the "thorn in my side"[35] that Paul spoke of in Corinthians. I accepted it as the way that God had made me, my emotional physiology. I would surrender to the thought that this was as good as it gets and embrace it. I would "submit and live,"[36] as the writer of Hebrews advises as a response to trials.

Illusive Happiness

But deep down, *I just wanted to be happy*. When you are happy, everything is better. It's like being in love. When you are in love, everything becomes bearable - the traffic, an unreasonable boss, deadlines, exams, complicated relations, you name it, all takes on a rosy hue.

I found solace in the book of Ecclesiastes, (which is

---

[35] 2 Corinthians 12:7
[36] Hebrews 12:9

admittedly hard to read in its entirety without some resolve on behalf of the reader.) In it, Solomon records his experiences with uncomfortable frankness. He strips life down to its bare bones and observes it without hype or spin. He considers the unfairness and inequality of life and the seeming meaninglessness of wisdom. He goes so far as to say that the dead are better off than the living and better still, those who have never been born.[37] If you were not depressed before reading the book, you are sure to be well on your way after reading it!

Solomon seemed to be an idealist, who became disillusioned *despite* his remarkable endeavors. His wounding didn't come from obvious trauma but rather from the apparent meaninglessness of life. His conclusion to all his observations does bring some relief, "Now all has been heard; here is the conclusion of the matter: Fear God and keep His commandments for this is the duty of all mankind."[38] He concludes that as real and as pressing as life on earth is, all that matters is eternal; so fear God and keep his commands. It's interesting how some come to this conclusion through suffering and others through a "blessed" life. God truly knows what each of us needs.

---

[37] Ecclesiastes 4:2-3
[38] Ecclesiastes 12:13

In amongst his melancholic meanderings, Solomon speaks of a happiness from God. "To the person who pleases him, God gives wisdom, knowledge and happiness."[39] He speaks of the man who pleases God, seldom reflecting on the days of his life "because God keeps him occupied with gladness of heart."[40]

I longed for this God-given happiness, this kind of mental pre-occupation. According to Solomon, you won't find it in wisdom or temporary pleasure. It's not found in wealth or reputation, or even in the absence of struggles. It's a gift, given by God, "For without *him*, who can eat or find enjoyment?"[41]

Is There a Way Out?

The Hebrew word for happiness is *Simcha*. It is the same word used in Thessalonians, "rejoice always..."[42] or be happy always. It is not the kind of *Simcha* that comes from a pep talk or positive thinking. The Bible is speaking of a happiness that holds firm in the face of gale force winds.

---

[39] Ecclesiastes 2:26

[40] Ecclesiastes 5:20

[41] Ecclesiastes 2:25 (emphasis added)

[42] 1 Thessalonians 5:16 (emphasis added)

The first step in getting this kind of happiness, is understanding what takes it away. In his book *How to Win over Depression*, Tim LaHaye asserts, "Nothing produces depression faster or more deeply than self-pity."[43] In fact, he claims that it is one of the *primary* causes of depression. This idea surprised me as I had heard depression mostly defined as "anger turned inward".

Initially, I took offense at what Le Haye was suggesting. I considered myself a strong, independent and productive person. I didn't give into self-pity. I got hurt, wounded even, sad at times, genuinely sad, but I never feel sorry for myself. I was tempted to put the book down, discarding it atop a pile of Christian pop-psychology, but instead decided to meditate on it. It didn't take long for me to recognize the self-pity in my thinking. It had just been well camouflaged in genuine difficulties and justifications so that I hadn't seen it for what it was. I realized that I felt sorry for myself; a lot. I was an idealist, I had been wounded, and feeling sorry for myself was the obvious next step.

Can you relate?

---

[43] LaHaye, Tim. How to Win over Depression, Updated and Expanded. (1996) Zondervan

Perhaps like me, you don't consider yourself as someone who gives in to self-pity. You view it as a pathetic, unproductive emotion and you may even spurn it in others. Fair enough, but see if you can recognize it in these commonplace thoughts:

"That was a long night, and I didn't sleep well, the dog next door kept barking. Why of all the nights? I am so tired and I need to be at work early today. Why does this always happen to me?

Man, it's so hot. When will it rain? It's so cold, when will this winter end? I am not feeling well; my throat is sore; why does my throat have to be sore when I have an important week?

Why do I have to have this chronic illness? I would like to do so much more; can't God see that?

I have no money. Why do other people have money when I don't have money? Why am I the only one?

Why does the boss always ask me to do this? Why can't somebody else do it?

Why do I struggle with this sin? Why is it so hard for me to be spiritual; others seem to be spiritual and overcome their sin so easily? What's wrong with me?

Why aren't people grateful for what I do for them? I make such an effort with people but people don't seem to make much effort with me?

Why do people have to be so sensitive? I have tried I have done my bit. Why me? Why is this happening? Why is God doing this to me, what have I done wrong? Why am I still single? Its just not fair."

And it goes on and on, you get the idea.

Very rarely did I ever verbalize thoughts like these. They were like a soundtrack playing in the background while I did life. The English Oxford Dictionary defines self-pity as: "excessive, self-absorbed unhappiness over one's own troubles."[44]

It's not just feeling sad about something, and it's not the normal grief after a loss; it's an all-consuming state where you feel like you are the only one suffering and no-one understands. It's a self-focused breeding pot for resentment.

Dealing With It

LaHaye proposes that identifying self-pity in your thinking is the first step in dealing with it. The second step is to treat it as sin. If I had replaced self-pity with lustful thoughts in my mind, I would have eradicated my depressed mood years ago. I have zero-tolerance with

---

[44] www.oed.com

lustful thinking. These thoughts are not allowed in my mind. I study out verses on purity; I pray, I fast if necessary and get open with a faithful friend or two.

I had never treated self-pity this way. If I ever did admit to feeling sorry for myself, I would allow the thoughts to linger like an understanding friend, ready to take my side of the argument. Little did I realize that I was entertaining a deadly enemy that would soon leave me feeling hopeless. The author and playwright, John Gardner put it like this: "Self-pity is easily the most destructive of the non-pharmaceutical narcotics; it is addictive, gives momentary pleasure and separates the victim from reality." [45]

So, if self-pity is a sinful mindset that steals happiness, how do we overcome it? Positive thinking? Telling yourself not to feel sorry for yourself even though you are genuinely experiencing a challenging time? How does one maintain authenticity and get rid of self-pity?

LaHaye proposes that the way to overcome self-pity is found in First Thessalonians,

---

[45] Gardner, John. The Art of Fiction: Notes on Craft for Young Writers. (1991). Vintage Publishers

"rejoice always, pray continually, give thanks in all circumstances; for this is God's will for you in Christ."[46]

We are to give thanks in *all circumstances*, not just in the good times. We are to give thanks for our difficulties, struggles, illnesses, rebellious children, lack of sleep, ineffectiveness, fatigue, childlessness, issues with weight, lack of money, aging bodies, loneliness, relational conflict, and work stress... The thing that makes you feel sorry for yourself is the *very thing* you are to thank God for. This seems to go against everything natural! I suppose that's the point. What comes naturally is complaining, arguing and self-pity. God is calling us to be thankful at our lowest points as well as at our highest.

A Sad King and a Glad Prophet

A potential trigger for self-pity is when, in your mind, you have done the right thing. You have given your best, acted reasonably and even compromised for the sake of harmony, but the results do not turn out as you imagined. Let's take a quick look at two biblical characters to whom

---

[46] 1 Thessalonians 5:16 -17 (emphasis added)

66

this happened and see the difference in their responses and where those responses led.

In First Kings 21, we witness King Ahab giving into a major bout of self-pity.[47] It was embarrassing that a king of Israel should behave in this way. He was sulking and sullen, and like a three-year-old child, ended up lying on his bed refusing to eat. What in his thinking could have possibly justified his actions?

As we know from the previous chapter on Elijah, Ahab was a very evil king. He was used to getting his way by whatever means necessary. It appears from this story that, for once, he had actually tried to do the right thing; to be fair and reasonable in his dealing with one of his citizens. He must have felt pretty good about himself when he made Naboth his "honorable" business proposal. When Naboth refused his deal, he fell apart and felt entirely justified in his self-piteous behavior. The trap of expecting life to be fair can seriously trip us, idealists, up. While I can't say that I have ever ended up sullen on my bed refusing food, I can certainly relate to the self-pity and sulking at perceived injustices.

In the book of Daniel, we read of Daniel's response to being unfairly treated. He was a Jew exiled in a foreign

---

[47] 1 Kings 21:1-7

country. Despite having to work under the authority of a pagan king, he was a man of integrity, upright in all he did. The Bible says that he distinguished himself above all the other administrators in Babylon. This galled them, and so they came up with a plan to discredit him before the king and have him executed. Their plan was to make it illegal, on penalty of death, to pray to any "god" other than the king. How would Daniel respond? Discouraged, disappointed at the injustice of doing right and yet penalized for it? Surely a little self-pity would be understandable in his circumstance?

A Different Response

The Bible tells of how, on learning of the decree, Daniel went home to his upstairs room. Three times a day he got down on his knees and prayed, *giving thanks* to his God, just as he had done before.[48] What an outstanding example. Rather than feel sorry for himself, Daniel continued to thank God in *all* circumstances.

———

It always amazes me how when you learn something new, God gives you an opportunity to put it into practice right away. We had just had new cupboards installed. I

---

[48] Daniel 6:1-10

loved the new cupboard smell and couldn't help smiling every time I walked past them. Shortly after their installation we noticed a gentle hissing sound coming from the cupboards. It sounded like water seeping from a broken pipe. We had plumbers in to no avail. After about a month, the mystery of the hissing cupboards was solved as two termites pushed their way through the cupboard's paint facade, exposing what had been going on behind the scene.

Thank God for Termites!

In South Africa, our homes are made of brick, so while there was no danger to the overall structure of the house, the critters were eating our newly installed cupboards! I was tempted to feel angry, discouraged and disappointed but decided to put the Bible's advice into practice. I thanked God for the termites. I thanked him that they had eaten our cupboards, I thanked him that it reminded me that this is not our home and that our home is in heaven; *where there are no termites!* Amazingly, what would have usually been a trigger for self-pity and subsequent depression was stopped in its tracks, and I experienced no dip in mood. This is a silly example for illustrative purposes, but over the past years, I have applied this advice consistently every time I have been tempted to feel sorry for myself - with remarkable results. I still get sad and moody but I am happy to say that the darkness of dysthymia has been kept at bay. (For some reading this, you may have experienced or are experiencing wounds that are still deep and raw, regardless of the amount of time that has passed. We would highly recommend that you read Shapiro and Shapiro's book, Rejoice Always and if necessary, seek professional help. There is no reason to struggle alone. There is so much hope. Don't allow fear, a stigma or even your own pride stop you from getting the help you need.)

As we close off this chapter, I encourage you to take some time to think of the things that make you unhappy. Maybe you need to write them down and see if you can recognize any self-pity in your thoughts. I want to encourage you to start thanking God for these things. Admittedly you may start by thanking him through clenched teeth, and it may even feel inauthentic (something we idealists hate), but let me encourage you to persevere.

God knows what is good for us; he made us and his Word can be fully trusted. Fear God, obey him and do it his way, even if his way doesn't always make sense. Slowly your jaw will loosen up, and you will be amazed at the freedom true surrender brings!

A Case Study: Peter

*A man gazing on the stars is proverbially
at the mercy of the puddles in the road.*
Alexander Smith

When one thinks of idealists in the New Testament,
Peter is surely the first to come to mind. He wore his heart
on his sleeve and was as genuine as a person could be. He
wasn't trying to be politically correct or to fit in. He was
who he was, warts and all. Through the gospels we get a
documented journey of how his idealism turned to faith.
Later in the books of First and Second Peter we are made
privy to the results of that faith 30 years on.

Peter, like Elijah, was on the Mount of Transfiguration.
But unlike Elijah, he was not particularly helpful. The
wonder of the experience caught him off guard; it terrified
and humbled him. While Elijah was a man at the end of
his faith journey, Peter was at the start of his and God, in
his wisdom, wanted them both there.

Enjoying the Idealism

We are first introduced to Peter in John chapter one
when his brother Andrew brings him to Jesus. On hearing

that Jesus might be the long-awaited Messiah, Peter's imagination was stirred, and so he dropped everything and followed.

News of this intriguing new prophet spread quickly across the Galilean countryside. He was driving out demons, performing miracles and delivering rousing messages. He ate at Peter's house and even healed his mother-in-law. One evening, the whole town gathered outside Peter's house. Everyone had come to his house to see his houseguest. The next morning, Jesus was nowhere to be found. Startled, Peter searched for him. He was not about to let this once in a lifetime opportunity pass him by. On finding Jesus, he exclaimed, "everyone is looking for you!"

The excitement in the region must have been tangible. In a world without TV, the Internet or movie theaters, storytelling was entertainment. The stories of Jesus must have taken on a life of their own as they passed from person to person. This small rural community was experiencing an upheaval and Peter was right in the middle of it. Overnight, Peter, this lowly fisherman, had become the companion of a local celebrity.

As he journeyed with Jesus, Peter experienced incredible things. He was at the wedding in Cana when

Jesus changed water into wine. He witnessed miraculous healings, people raised from the dead and demons sent packing. Twice he was a part of the feeding of thousands, and twice he had to clean up after the crowds had left. On one occasion, he watched in amazement as Jesus calmed a storm, on another he walked on water as Jesus calmed him. In-between it all, were the life-changing sermons, lessons and countless late night conversations.

Perceived invincibility

Jesus' evident disregard for the Pharisees may have been especially appealing to Peter. Pharisees had most likely looked down on him his whole life. A cursing fisherman was not accepted or even liked by the religious crowd. They weren't exactly in the same social circles. On one Sabbath, while walking through fields, Peter and the other disciples picked some grain. Indignant, the Pharisees challenged Jesus on it. I imagine the disciples must have swallowed hard. *"Sorry Jesus, old habits, didn't mean to discredit you."*

But instead of rebuking the disciples, Jesus turned and rebuked the Pharisees! It happened another time. The Pharisees pointed out that some of his disciples were eating food with unclean hands. Again Jesus defended the disciples and rebuked the Pharisees.

This lowly, irreligious fisherman must have felt invincible. It was him and God against the world and nothing was going to stop them! The call to follow Jesus was all Peter could have asked for and more.

No Talk of Suffering

As they traveled along, Jesus repeatedly warned Peter and the others that it wasn't always going to be easy. Trials (literal and figurative) lay ahead. For our idealistic Peter, talk of suffering, rejection, and failure confused him. This kind of negativity should not be coming from a dead-raising, water-walking, storm-calming, world-changing leader. At one point he even took Jesus aside and began to rebuke him.[49] It was not one of Peter's finest moments. He must have cringed in embarrassment when he looked back on the conversation years later. He had rebuked the Son of God! What had he been thinking? But it exposed his naivety and inexperience in spiritual warfare.

When Jesus predicted that all of the disciples would fall away, Peter insisted, "Even if all fall away, I will not."[50] He even went as far as to say that he would rather die than

---

[49] Matthew 16:2-22
[50] Mark 14:27-31

disown Jesus. How could he ever disown such a glorious leader? Why would he ever leave such an awe-inspiring, radical, victorious movement? He was living in an idealistic world that was starting to make sense and him falling away was not part of it.

The Garden of Disillusionment

After the Passover meal, Jesus and the disciples entered the Garden of Gethsemane.[51] It would be for Jesus the place of his ultimate surrender to God's will. But for Peter, Gethsemane marked the beginning of the end. The place where his world came crashing down around him, the olive grove where his bubble burst.

Imagine the thoughts racing through Peter's head as Jesus was being arrested; "Come on Jesus; you are here to change the world. You can't let this insignificant horde stand in your way. Jesus, do something! What is happening? There was no way that Jesus was going to allow this. I know Jesus is going to stop this and perform another miracle."

The perfect world that had made so much sense to him, now *made no sense at all.* Why was Jesus allowing this to

---

[51] Mark 14:32

75

happen? Why wasn't he defending himself? In his panic and confusion, Peter takes it upon himself to save the day! He draws out a sword and strikes the servant of the high priest, cutting off his ear. But Jesus doesn't commend him; no, he stops him and tells him to put away his sword. **"Shall I not drink the cup the Father has given me?"**[52]

"Drink the cup?

What cup?

I have seen you walk on water and raise the dead – this small group is nothing for you to deal with.

Do something, Jesus!

Defend yourself! Defend us!

You can, I believe!

Don't let this happen!!

Make it stop!"

But Jesus doesn't make it stop; he doesn't defend himself, and he doesn't defend them. He allowed himself to be arrested and taken away. So Peter ran away. He would sneak back later to watch what would happen, but he followed at a safe distance. Before the night was over he would deny his best friend, his Lord and Messiah three

---

[52] John 18:10-11

times. At one point, to defend himself, he claimed, "I don't know *the man*".[53] How different from the days when he called Jesus the *Son of God.*

When the rooster crowed, Jesus, knowing of Peter's betrayal, turned to look at him. Peter's heart broke.[54] This tough fisherman sobbed in Jerusalem's dusty streets. But he wasn't crying for Jesus or for the brutal treatment Jesus was about to endure. He was crying for himself. He nursed his wounds while his Lord hung on a cross. Jesus must have looked out from that cross, longing to see his friend's face in the hostile crowd. But Peter was not there. The time Jesus needed his friend most; he was nowhere to be seen. Peter's new reality was too painful to bear; he could only see his own pain and fear. All his hopes and expectations had come to nothing and he was deeply disappointed. His idealism fell hopelessly short of true faith. Isaiah put it like this: "If you do not stand firm in your faith, you will not stand at all."[55]

Idealism is NOT Faith

Growing up, I (Irene) thought that idealism and faith

---

[53] Matthew 26:74 (emphasis added)

[54] Luke 22:60-62

[55] Isaiah 7:9

were the same thing. I went to a church that taught that faith was all you needed to bring about the prosperous life you desired. If your prayers were not answered, then you were the problem. You lacked faith. I came to realize that not only is this teaching fraught with doctrinal errors; it is actually a breeding ground for despondency. No matter how hard you believe, if your prayers aren't answered, it exposes you as a pseudo-Christian that God won't listen to. The problem with this doctrine is that it lacks a balanced biblical view. While the Bible does say, "ask and you will receive"[56], it also describes a lowly widow who had to persevere in her prayers against an unjust judge. If unanswered prayers reflect a lack of faith where does that put Jesus who begged God to take away his cup of his suffering? Something is fundamentally wrong with this theology. It is idealistic and potentially damaging.

Let us consider a few other differences between idealism and faith:

- Idealists are brave talkers BUT a person of faith is actually brave. They do what is hard and requires courage. They step out of their comfort zones.
- Idealists can be entitled in their requests before God and are surprised when he doesn't answer

---

[56] John 16:24

how and when they think he should BUT a person of faith approaches God with humility, trusting that God's will is good, pleasing and perfect.

- An idealist loves to dream and come up with grand schemes. Seldom do they invest in the hard work that it would take to bring their plans to fruition BUT a person of faith dreams, plans, and acts.

- An idealist wants to quit when it gets tough BUT a person of faith perseveres through trials.

- An idealist sets their hope on a specific outcome BUT a person of faith sets their hope on God, believing that whatever the outcome, God is working. They open many doors and allow God to close the ones he wants closed.

- An idealist believes that no one should be hurt in the kingdom of God BUT the person of faith understands that we are a group of sinners trying our best. When we hurt each other, God has given us the tools to overcome it.

- Idealists try to avoid or distract (through sport, holidays, entertainment, hobbies) the chaos of life BUT the person of faith accepts the fallen state of the world and seeks God in it.

Our goal must be to become people of faith.

The Essence of Idealism

Before we close this chapter, let us revisit the interaction where Peter rebukes Jesus. Embarrassing for Peter, a lesson for us.

> From that time on Jesus began to explain to his disciples that he must go to Jerusalem and suffer many things at the hands of the elders, the chief priests and the teachers of the law, and that he must be killed and on the third day be raised to life. Peter took him aside and began to rebuke him. "Never, Lord!" he said. "This shall never happen to you!" Jesus turned and said to Peter, "**Get behind me, Satan! You are a stumbling block to me; you do not have in mind the concerns of God, but merely human concerns.**" Then Jesus said to his disciples, "Whoever wants to be my disciple must deny themselves and take up their cross and follow me. For whoever wants to save their life will lose it, but whoever loses their life for me will find it."[57]

Here we have that awkward moment where Peter rebukes Jesus for talking about suffering. What's interesting is how Jesus responds to Peter's faulty

---

[57] Matthew 16:21-25 (emphasis added)

reasoning. "Get behind me, Satan! You are a *stumbling block* to me; you do not have in mind the concerns of God, but merely human concerns."

The NLT puts it like this:

"Get away from me, Satan! You are a *dangerous trap* to me. You are seeing things merely from a human point of view, not from God's." [58]

Peter received a stiff rebuke from Jesus. He rebuked Peter's worldly, idealistic view where "human concerns" take center stage. But how easy is it for *us* to think the same way? It comes so naturally for us to make our comfort and wellbeing our number one priority. Rather than the concerns of God, we can so easily focus on what we think will make us feel happy and fulfilled. Our plans, our dreams. This is the essence of idealism.

What we must understand is that not only is idealism *not faith*, it is, in fact, a stumbling block to faith - a hindrance to faith and a dangerous trap. While we may start out with natural youthful idealism, we must mature beyond it. We are meant to outgrow it, like a worn pair of jeans from our childhood. It must be replaced by a faith

---

[58] Emphasis added

that is deeply rooted in God's Word. We cannot let it stunt our faith or sabotage our beliefs and hopes.

The good news is that Peter's story didn't end at the wounding. In fact, *his best years came after the wounding.* He journeyed from being an idealist to becoming a man of incredible faith and the first leader of the first-century church.

In the next chapter we are going to study First Peter and see what this faith in action looked like. Amazingly Peter uses the word suffering 21 times in First Peter alone.

Let us not lose sight of the life to which we have been called, a life where God can do immeasurably more than all we can ask or imagine. But let us move onto maturity to accept not only the times when we are on the top of the mountain and but equally embrace the times in the valley!

Now that is true *Faith*!

From Idealism to Faith - First Peter

"...by His wounds you have been healed."
1 Peter 2:24

When we are young, life seems simple. The future is obvious and predictable; it's all clearly mapped out in our minds. We expect to take a smooth ride from point A to B. We think, "I am going to finish school, get a boyfriend or girlfriend, go to college, graduate in four years, get married, have a successful career and two kids (ideally twins). Then later in life, I will travel the world and retire, preferably near the beach or in the mountains."

In reality, our life path is never that straight or smooth.

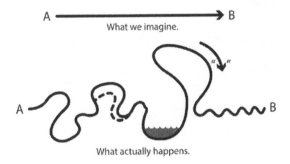

A ————————————————→ B
What we imagine.

A ~~~~~~~~~~~~~~~~~~~~~ B
What actually happens.

What we imagined and what actually happens can look very different. Life can throw us many unexpected curveballs.

Themba's Story

Themba, a Christian from the Soweto Region of the Johannesburg Church of Christ understands that all too well. As a recovering wounded idealist, we wanted to share his story: "I can relate to Elijah and Peter. Having become a Christian at the age of 16, I wanted to change the world. I believed that God had handpicked me for a noble purpose and that I was destined for something great. I shared my faith with everything that moved. I was known in high school as a religious zealot. That never bothered me. I guess I thought of myself as God's chosen man and the comments of people around me validated that belief.

When I entered the full-time ministry in 1999, it re-affirmed that I was born for something greater than myself. I loved working in the ministry. It gave me a sense of direction and purpose.

In 2002 my older brother died. I had never experienced the death of someone close to me before. It broke me. I could not pray or read my bible for a long time. I did not understand God. It felt like He had abandoned me. But as an idealist, I once again threw myself into what I loved best, the ministry. Serving as an intern, I worked under several different leaders. At first, things went well under their leadership, but in time, for different reasons, each leader ended up facing life-changing spiritual crises. Though it was difficult for me to see spiritual heroes struggle, I soldiered on. On the romantic front, I was convinced that it was God's will for me to date and marry a certain beautiful, spiritual woman. It made sense. We shared the same dreams, we had similar convictions and had been friends since our campus days. It was a mild day in April 2007 when I got the call that she had been killed in a car accident. We were meant to go on a date that week. I was shattered. It felt like God was out to get me. I wanted to die.

In 2008 I was asked to temporarily lead a small church in another city in South Africa. My heart felt refreshed and my vision re-ignited. But just as it started to feel like I had found a new home, a year later, I was back in Soweto. Tragically that same year, my younger brother died. I was finished. It took me well over two years to recover and sense a glimmer of hope again. In 2011, despite my limping faith I took over leading the Soweto region. The truth is that I was not honest with myself or those around me at how disillusioned I was with my life. I wanted to be that strong, optimistic leader that I had envisioned in my mind and so I forged on. In 2013 my father was diagnosed with cancer. No words. Then in 2014, under my leadership, the Soweto region started falling apart. A year later I chose to step out of the ministry. It felt like everything I had worked so hard for was gone. I was no longer God's chosen. I felt like King Saul, rejected by God. I was deeply wounded."

Like Themba, we can feel like life is not all we hoped or imagined it would be. The challenge for us is to resist becoming cynical and jaded when we are disappointed. Our goal is to trade youthful idealism and wishful thinking in for true faith. It is the only way to make it through the inevitable hard times.

In the previous chapter, we looked at a few differences between idealism and faith. These are summarized in the following chart:

Idealist	Person of faith
Brave talker	Brave
Entitled before God	Humble before God
Dreams more than acts	Acts

Wants to quit when it gets tough	Perseveres through trials
Sets hope on a specific outcome	Sets hope on God's will
Thinks there should be no conflict in God's kingdom/family	Understands that we hurt one another but God provides us with love and forgiveness
Avoids or distracts from the chaos of life	Accepts the chaos of life and looks for God in it.

Despite Peter's rocky beginnings, he traded his idealism in for true faith and was chosen by God to lead the first-century church.

Brave Hearts

When we first meet Peter in the gospels, he is in his late 20s. We meet up with him again in First Peter; thirty years later. When he wrote First Peter, the church was undergoing a time of severe persecution. The purpose of the letter was to strengthen exiled Christians whose lives were in jeopardy. Up until then, the Roman government had, for the most part, left the Christians alone. Christianity was not seen as a new religion but rather as a sect under the umbrella of Judaism. In adherence to their "nation conquering policy," the Romans allowed the conquered nation to continue the worship of their own gods. The one condition was that these religions be state approved.[59] When it became clear that Christianity was not another Jewish sect but a separate religion, it became by law, illegal. Ardent to stamp out any potential civil unrest, persecution by the Romans started in earnest.

Rumors and slander about Christianity were rampant.[60] When Emperor Nero saw an opportunity to use the negative sentiment towards Christians to his advantage, he burnt down the slums of Rome and blamed the Christians. Many died in the fire, and the persecution of the Christians took a grave turn for the worse. The Christians were tortured and killed en masse.

Given this context, how does Peter, a former idealist encourage these Christians who were living under such dire circumstances? Would he tell them to make a run for it like he did in the dreaded Garden of his disillusionment

---

[59] Barclay, William. The Letters Of James and Peter. (1976) Westminster Press

[60] For example Christians were accused of cannibalism (eating the flesh and blood of their Lord), of having incestuous relationships (marrying a brother or sister), of being subversive to the government (by proclaiming Jesus and not the Emperor as Lord) and of promoting hatred of mankind by loving "their God" above anyone else.

or would he encourage them to stand and fight for their faith? Let's look at a few of verses.

In all this you greatly *rejoice*, though now for a little while you may have had to *suffer* grief in all kinds of trials. These have come so that the proven genuineness of your faith—of greater worth than gold, which perishes even though refined by fire— may result in praise, glory and honor when Jesus Christ is revealed.[61]

But if you *suffer* for doing good and you endure it, this is *commendable* before God. To this you were called, because Christ suffered for you, leaving you an example that you should follow in his steps.[62]

But even if you should *suffer* for what is right, you are *blessed*. "Do not fear their threats; do not be frightened."[63]

Do not be surprised at the fiery ordeal that has come on you to test you, as though something strange were happening to you. But *rejoice* inasmuch as you participate in the *sufferings* of

---

[61] 1 Peter 1:6-9 (emphasis added)
[62] 1 Peter 2:21 (emphasis added)
[63] 1 Peter 3:13-14 (emphasis added)

Christ, so that you may be overjoyed when his glory is revealed.[64]

Be alert and of **sober mind**. Your enemy the devil prowls around like a roaring lion looking for someone to devour. Resist him, **standing firm** in the faith, because you know that the family of believers throughout the world is undergoing the same kind of sufferings.[65]

How different this Peter is to the man we read about in the gospels! He went from being indignant when Jesus spoke of suffering to referring to it 21 times in the book of First Peter alone. While suffering had caused the younger man to falter in his faith and abandon his Lord at the cross, the man of faith now encourages the Christians to not "be surprised," that they "were called to times of suffering," and are "blessed," "refined," and should "rejoice." All this was coming from the conviction that their faith, of greater worth than gold, was being strengthened and proven genuine through suffering.

Finding God in The Chaos

If Peter had remained a wounded idealist, he probably

---

[64] 1 Peter 4:12-13 (emphasis added)
[65] 1 Peter 5:8-9 (emphasis added)

would have told them to make a run for it, to get out while they still could. Maybe he would have expressed his confusion at why God was allowing them to suffer these atrocities. He would encourage them to beg God to save them from the situation or at least pray for a change of government! But instead, he calls them to set their hope on what is eternal and not what is temporary. In a less than ideal world he urges them to find God in the chaos.

Today, few of us live under threat for our faith. We don't have Roman soldiers arriving at our doors ready to drag us off to the arenas. Even so, life on earth is still pretty chaotic. The world is filled with so much evil and hurt. We don't have to look far to see its effects. Broken lives, marriages, and families surround us. Murder, pornography, hatred, racism, and abuse are commonplace. We have politicians who lie and leaders who seek personal gain. Injustice and corruption have become a way of life. Around the world, there are civil wars, displaced refugees, disease, and poverty. There are extremes in the weather and the threat of terror attacks. Besides everything else, we have concerns about our futures – our families, our spouses, our children, our finances, our friendships and our careers. So while a Roman soldier may not be knocking at your front door, *really, he doesn't have to.* Life is less than ideal.

Peter's encouragement to our first-century brothers and sisters can be our encouragement.

Embrace the Word of God

Peter encourages these brave saints to rely on God's word.

> For you have been born again, not of perishable seed, but of imperishable, through the living and enduring word of God. For, "All people are like grass, and all their glory is like the flowers of the field; the grass withers and the flowers fall, **but the word of the Lord endures forever.**"[66]

> Like newborn babies, **crave pure spiritual milk**, so that by it you may grow up in your salvation.[67]

If you Google the words "I feel sad," you will find references to almost every psychological, holistic, spiritual and alternative discipline out there. "Five ways to feel happy, 30 ways to improve your mood, coping with depression…" WikiHow's 4-step plan is to journal, laugh out loud, have a good cry and see the bigger picture. While

---

[66] 1 Peter 1:23-25 (emphasis added)
[67] 1 Peter 2:2 (emphasis added)

these platforms may be helpful at times, it becomes all too easy to turn to them for help instead of the Word of God.

In today's media obsessed world, self-help forums, pithy Pinterest sayings, and the latest pop-psychology can become what we depend on to get us through the day. What we need to recognize is that much of what is advocated to steady our lives has its basis in the Scriptures. Despite what modern "enlightened" experts will tell you, there is indeed nothing new under the sun. These experts are ultimately drawing on ancient wisdom and truth, all of which are found in God's word.

Consider the following examples:

- *The Power of Positive Thinking* was first presented to the world by Norman Vincent Peale in 1952, and yet 2000 years earlier Paul wrote to the Church in Philippi:

  Finally, whatever is true, whatever is noble, whatever is right, whatever is pure, whatever is lovely, whatever is admirable—if anything is excellent or praiseworthy—think about such things.[68]

---

[68] Philippians 4:8

- Mindfulness is another "modern" psychological process, incorporated into clinical psychology and psychiatry since the 1970s. Jon Kabat-Zinn is considered to have initiated its recent popularity in the West. At the risk of being simplistic, it advocates living in the present and reducing stress through meditation. Yet, Jesus told his followers two millennia earlier to not worry about tomorrow but rather to focus on today.[69] 1000 years before that, King David speaks of meditation repeatedly in the Psalms.

- Vulnerability and Shame have also become a talking point highlighted by the TED talk by Brene Brown.[70] It captured the hearts of Internet users worldwide with millions of views. And yet we read in Second Corinthians that we are to delight in our weakness and not try to cover them up[71]. James even calls Christians to confess their sins *to one another*[72]. It doesn't get more vulnerable than that.

---

[69] Matthew 6:25-34

[70] https://www.ted.com/talks/brene_brown_on_vulnerability

[71] 2 Corinthians 12:9-12

[72] James 5:16

- Or how about the mind-body connection
  model? It proposes that our emotions affect our
  health.[73] A new revelation? Not according to
  King Solomon who tells us in the Proverbs that,
  "A heart at peace gives life to the body, but
  envy rots the bones."[74]

It's as if movements like these have stumbled upon new
truths, when really they are as old as mankind itself. And
this wisdom, this eternal knowledge has been
painstakingly recorded in God's Word.

The Ultimate Weapon

The Bible is unlike any book you will ever read. It
describes itself as alive and powerful[75] and as the sword of
the Spirit[76]. By *it* and *it* alone can we demolish arguments
and strongholds that set themselves against the knowledge
of God. Through using God's Word, we are able to take
captive every thought and make it obedient to Christ.[77]
John tells us that Jesus is the Word of God in the flesh and

---

[73] https://plato.stanford.edu/entries/mental-causation/

[74] Proverbs 14:30

[75] Hebrews 4:12

[76] Ephesians 6:17

[77] 2 Corinthians 10:5

through the Word all things, seen and unseen, were made.[78] When Jesus himself was tempted, he used the Word to overcome Satan – not positive mantras or human reasoning. He quoted Scripture. He knew the Scriptures. They were memorized in his heart.[79]

There is only one eternal truth, and it is found in God's Word. It is the source of all life and all revelation. What a travesty when we take it for granted or feel like it's boring. If we are to overcome and be victorious in this life, we must consistently read and embrace God's Word, whether we feel like reading it or not. We have this discipline with eating. Most of us eat every day, whether we feel like eating or not. If we starve ourselves physically we feel fatigued, weak and irritable. The same is true spiritually. When we are *not* consistently feeding our souls on God's Word, we become weak, tired and irritable. Some of us are starved spiritually and don't even realize it. We can only fight spiritual battles with spiritual weapons. You will not overcome sin, negative emotions, guilt, or regret by applying worldly solutions to a spiritual problem.

---

[78] John 1:1-3
[79] Matthew 4:1-10

Idealists enjoy riding on "good vibes" and positive feelings. They must learn the discipline of reading and relying on the Word of God as the foundation of life.

Be Sober-Minded and Holy

The Oxford dictionary defines being sober-minded as, "serious, sensible, and composed." This is very different from the Peter we meet in the gospels and yet in First Peter he repeats the words three times.

> Therefore, with **minds** that are alert and **fully sober**, set your hope on the grace to be brought to you when Jesus Christ is revealed at his coming. As obedient children, do not conform to the evil desires you had when you lived in ignorance. But just as he who called you is holy, so be holy in all you do; for it is written: "Be holy, because I am holy."[80]

> The end of all things is near. Therefore be alert and of **sober mind** so that you may pray.[81]

> Be alert and of **sober mind**. Your enemy the devil prowls around like a roaring lion looking for someone to devour.[82]

---

[80] 1 Peter1: 13-16 (emphasis added)
[81] 1 Peter 4:7 (emphasis added)
[82] 1 Peter 5: 8 (emphasis added)

We are in a spiritual war. The enemy is circling, looking for someone to devour. While this vision is not something an idealist is likely to embrace, it is the spiritual reality. When we suffer or are wounded, the challenge is to respond in a sober-minded way. Our natural tendency is to distract from or avoid the pain, and sin and excessive behavior are easy and convenient ways; you don't even have to leave your house. Alcohol, drugs, nicotine, subscription painkillers, sleeping tablets, pornography, social media and gaming addiction, sexual acting out, extreme sports, overworking, constant holidays or fantasizing about it, over-spending, over-eating, and over-sleeping are some examples of easy distractions.
Peter calls us to abstain from all such sinful desires, which wage war on our souls.[83]

Themba's Story Continued

"I often caught myself being cynical or negative about life. The great sense of optimism and idealism had been pushed aside by the dread of something going wrong. I lived in constant fear. Other than my fear, I lived with debilitating regret. Regret for decisions and choices I had made. In fact, at times just thinking about it paralyzed me. I even experienced panic attacks. Regret is a harsh

---

[83] 1 Peter 2: 11-12

bedfellow. I guess that was what Peter felt, and why he wept so bitterly.

I started to rely on human wisdom to help bail me out of the emotional hell I found myself in. I turned to the internet and its numerous articles to address what I was facing in life, from depression to marital concerns. The Word of God stopped being my source of help and inspiration. I paid heavily for that. I honestly believe that if I had made the Word my best friend and obeyed it (rather than my feelings), I could have avoided most of my self-inflicted suffering. Although suffering is inevitable (to a large extent), some of it is completely avoidable if one bases their decisions on the Bible.

Peter could not reconcile his big dreams and the thought of suffering. Those two things were mutually exclusive for him. The early Christians suffered under Nero and many other like-minded lunatics. Suffering is inevitable when you live in a fallen world. This is a reality that I, as a radical idealist, have had a difficult time accepting. I had a hard time accepting the death of my loved ones, or even that all people will die in the end.

As one who is allergic to suffering, each difficult moment in my life would lead to many harmful habits, in an effort to medicate my pain. These would include watching television non-stop, to eating uncontrollably. I would do all these things because I just did not want to be sober about my situation. I wanted to escape, to feel better, and did not see the harm I was doing to my soul and health."

Turning Our Hearts Back to God

When our hearts ache, we want to find relief. At times we turn to sin and distraction when we need to turn to God. Peter directs our hearts to Jesus, the *only place* where we can find true peace and healing. It is by *his wounds* that we are healed.[84]

Our encouragement is that you will open up about how you have tried to avoid or distract from the pain of your disappointment. You know what you are running from. Stop running. Don't try to avoid the chaos. Get help to find God in the chaos. Satan lies to us and tells us to keep things under wraps. We say the light is our friend! As scary as it may seem to bring things into the light, the darkness is a lot scarier. The light is the safest place that you can be.

---

[84] 1 Peter 2: 24

A Cynic's Question and a Sage's Reply

If God is all loving then
he cannot be all powerful,
And if God is all powerful
then he cannot be all loving.
Lex Luthor

What is up with the Snake in the Garden?

If you are an idealist, the state of the world is particularly bothersome to you. And to be fair, it is pretty chaotic. In the previous chapter, we looked at how different life can be from what we hoped it would be, how different the world around us is to what we imagined it should be. Idealists grapple with this and wonder where to assign blame? Who is responsible for all this turmoil? Where can justice be meted out; the Man, the Woman, Satan?

Looking at human history, we see centuries of loss, tragedy, pain, suffering, wars, poverty, injustice, conflict, disease and death. Yes, there have been many marvels and achievements, but at its essence, the human journey on this planet has been one wrought with struggle.

If we take a step back, out of the limitations of the here and now, and view the human condition from the edge of time; from its initial inception, we find that all man's suffering can be pinpointed back to one decision.

One calculated risk.

One perilous choice.

So What Was It?

Was it Adam asking for a mate, or Eve talking to the serpent? Was it their lack of obedience, or them eating the forbidden fruit? Was it their decision to hide from God to cover up their shame?

No, these were consequences of that one decision.

The decision, *by God,* to allow the snake to be in the Garden of Eden in the first place, is what has caused all this pain and misery for humanity.

That Snake!

Think about it, if the snake had not been there, Adam and Eve would not have been tempted and mankind would not have fallen. We would not have been banned from the Garden of Eden; banished from the perfect world, the ideal world; the world an idealist longs for here on earth!

We can't place the blame on the man, the woman or the snake; we can only place the blame squarely on the shoulders of the one who was responsible for putting the snake in the Garden in the first place. On God! We have to turn our attention to God and contend with the ramifications.

It seems wrong even to write those words, and yet idealists and especially those who have been wounded, think about such things. Not many have the courage or maybe the gall to say them out loud, but you'll hear them clearly in the voice of cynics.

"How can a loving God ..?
If God exists why does he allow..?
If we look at the state of the world, God is either all loving or all powerful, he cannot be both, so which one is it..?
Why do people suffer..? Why is there so much evil..?"

Idealists are looking for answers, if not definitive answers; they want engagement on the topic. (If this is not the way you reason or the way you question the reality around you, you can't just cross your fingers and hope that those who do think this way will figure it out on their own, we must engage.) So how do we respond to such statements, to these allegations in which there seems to be some truth?

Here's a Thought

When a wounded idealist or cynic looks at the world, they ask how a loving God could allow this. They advocate love as the answer to creating a fair, free world. They talk about love, write poems about love and sing about love. Those who are older will remember the famous Beatle's song,

All you need is love, ba ba bada ba
All you need is love, ba ba bada ba
All you need is love, love
Love is all you need

Love is all you need. Love for the idealist, is the solution for all human ills. **But the truth is, idealists don't want anything to do with real love**. Here's the reality; in order to create the perfect, ideal world, what is required is *control* not love. Most idealists are not aware that they place a higher value on control than on love and it is to that end that they want the snake out of the Garden, for heaven's sake!

Here's the deal:

The Garden without the snake = **PERFECT CONTROL**
The Garden with the snake = **PERFECT LOVE**

No Snake!

If you take the snake out of the Garden, you would have no suffering, no pain, and no consequences. You would also have no choice or freedom. You would have no love or relationship, just containment. A perfectly controlled environment.

The snake in the Garden represents love at its most vulnerable. It offers choice and freedom, and with that, consequence. Despite what an idealist wants to believe, there are always strings attached when it comes to love. Anyone who has ever truly loved someone else, a high school sweetheart, a spouse, a child, a family member or friend – knows that it comes with its share of connection and joy but also heartache and pain. It is messy and complicated. It takes sacrifice, perseverance and at times self-denial to love another being. Love cost God his son; and it was this love that allowed him to take the risk, the gamble, to offer man the option to reject him and choose to believe the lies. All with devastating consequences.

The problem of pain and suffering is nothing new. It is not a modern conception or a recent notion. The biblical writers and prophets of old questioned and wrestled with its perplexing nature and apparent necessity.

One such writer describes his perspective of Israel's wandering but with a surprising conclusion. In Psalm 107 he describes groups of people who had suffered in different ways:

- Some **wandered** in desert **wastelands**, finding no way to a city where they could settle. They were **hungry** and **thirsty**, and **their lives ebbed away**. (vs. 4-5)

- Some sat in **darkness**, in **utter darkness**, prisoners **suffering** in iron chains, because they rebelled against God's commands and despised the plans of the Most High. So **he subjected them** to **bitter labor**; they **stumbled**, and there was no one to help. (vs. 10-12)

- Some became fools through their rebellious ways and **suffered affliction** because of their iniquities. They loathed all food and **drew near the gates of death**. (vs 17-18)

- Some went out on the sea in ships; they were merchants on the mighty waters. They saw the works of the Lord, his wonderful deeds in the deep. **For he spoke** and stirred up a tempest that lifted high the waves. They mounted up to the heavens and went down to the depths; in their peril **their courage melted away**. They **reeled**

and **staggered** like drunkards; **they were at their
wits' end.** (vs. 23-27)[85]

The Psalmist explains how every time they suffered
they would cry out to God and he would turn to them and
rescue them. He goes on to describe how God turned
rivers into a desert, flowing springs into thirsty ground,
and fruitful land into a salt waste. He tells of how God
humbled people by oppression, calamity and sorrow; and
poured out contempt on nobles making them wander in a
trackless waste.[86]

The modern reader may balk at the idea that God could
be behind these people's difficulties and trials and yet the
Psalmist ends his observation with these words:

> Let the one who is wise heed these things
> and ponder the loving deeds of the Lord.[87]

Let him who is WISE, ponder, consider, think about the
loving deeds of the Lord! Yes, most of us can recognize
the love of God in kindness shown by saving people from
their trials, but it is the truly wise, the sages amongst us,
that can recognize the love of God in allowing them to

---

[85] Emphasis added
[86] Psalm 107:33-40
[87] Psalm 107:43

face the trials in the first place. The truly wise see God. A God who gives us choice, even if it means rejecting him. A God willing and wanting to rescue us over and over again when *our* choices end up harming us.

Consider the following:

The Cynic proposes: If God created everything, then he created evil, which means that God is evil.

The Sage replies: Was cold created? In fact cold does not exist. According to the laws of physics, what we consider as cold is in reality the <u>absence of heat</u>.

What about darkness? Was it created? Darkness does not exist either. We can study light, but not darkness. Darkness is in reality the <u>absence of light</u>.

So was evil created? No, it is just like darkness and cold. God did not create evil. Evil is the result of what happens when man does not have God's love present in his heart.

<u>Evil is the absence of God.</u>

Author Unknown

The state of the world distresses God. He is equally torn up by the war, poverty, hatred and suffering that he sees.

He Never Created It

He devises ways to alleviate it, prevent it, interfere with it, but never control it. In his article, *Is God in Control?* Doug Schaefer contends that:

"God has created a world for us governed by laws, both physical and spiritual. Those things are constant. Gravity always pulls down and lying is always a sin, the sun rises in the East and love never fails. But what if they were not constant? What if God did manipulate every situation attempting to make everything alright regardless of our actions? Malachi 3:6-7 says that God set things up this way so that we would not be destroyed. Imagine waking up in the morning, not knowing whether or not fire would burn you or if gravity was going to work that day. What if there were situations where it was alright to lie or where sex outside of marriage was acceptable? It would be chaos! Much of the world operates under these 'conditional' morals and look at the mess it is in. No, our God has lovingly given us freedom. But with that freedom comes a heavy responsibility to seek out God's will and do the right thing."[88]

---

[88] www.douglasjacoby.com/q-a-0429-is-god-in-control-by-doug-shaefer/

Ultimately God wants us to be in heaven with him. It is the idealist's Utopia, Paradise, Shangri-La, the quintessential nirvana. But God wants us to *want* to be there, not because we have to, but because we choose to. If temporary suffering here on earth might mean that we turn to him, he will allow it. It is not because he is trying to control us or hurt us, quite the contrary, it is *because* he loves us.

This topic is far from fully developed or discussed but through this chapter we want to open a doorway to further consideration into such matters. Many far greater minds than ours have contemplated the meaning of life and the complexity of suffering, and to that end we suggest the following books for further reading.

Helpful books

The Problem of Pain by C.S. Lewis
A Grief Observed by C.S. Lewis
Disappointment With God by Philip Yancey
Where Is God When It Hurts? by Philip Yancey
Suffering and the Sovereignty of God by John Piper

Faithful Realism

The bravest are surely those
who have the clearest vision of what is
before them, glory and danger alike, and
yet not withstanding go out to meet it.

Thucydides

If a pessimist sees the glass as half empty, the idealist as half full, and the realist as a glass with water in it; the faithful realist sees the opportunity to refill it.

Idealism is not faith. But neither is realism. Our goal is to be faithful realists, not simply realists, filled with practicality, able to state the obvious but devoid of vision. Faithful realists, people able to see reality through a God-lens. Men and women of courage determined to advance despite the facts, bold dreamers grounded in God's will.

The Bible defines faith as "the confidence in what we hope for and assurance of what we do not see."[89]

While the visionary characteristic of idealism hints at faith, it fundamentally lacks what is required for faith. The question then to ask is: how does an idealist transition to

---

[89] Hebrews 11:1

111

faithful realism and circumvent the enticing lure of cynicism when disappointed?

A study of people of faith in the Bible, reveals an essential characteristic in faith formation. John the Baptist, the Roman centurion, the leper, the widow, the bleeding woman, the thief on the cross, Job, Shadrach, Meshach and Abednego, Abraham, David and the Hebrews 11 "Hall of Famers" all had one quality in common.

hu·mil·i·ty

The dictionary defines humility as "a modest view of one's own importance."[90]

In his aptly entitled book, *It's Not About Me,* Max Lucado redirects the reader to the essence of a God-centered life:

"What Copernicus did for earth, God does for our souls. Tapping the collective shoulder of humanity, he points to the Son – his Son – and says, 'Behold the center of it all.' When God looks at the center of the universe, he doesn't look at you. When heaven's stagehands direct the spotlight toward the star of the show, I need no sunglasses. No light

---

[90] www.dictionary.com

falls on me. Lesser orbs, that's us. Appreciated. Valued.
Loved dearly. But central? Essential? Pivotal? Nope.
Sorry. Contrary to the Ptolemy within us, the world
doesn't revolve around us. Our comfort is not God's
priority. If it is, something's gone awry. If we are the
marquee event, how do we explain flat-earth challenges
like death, disease, slumping economies, or rumbling
earthquakes? If God exists to please us, then shouldn't we
always be pleased? … Perhaps our place is not the center
of the universe. God does not exist to make a big deal out
of us. We exist to make a deal out of him. It's not about
you. It's not about me. It's all about him…They all told us
it was, didn't they? Weren't we urged to look out for
number one? Find our place in the sun? Make a name for
ourselves? We thought self-celebration would make us
happy… The God-centered life works. And it rescues us
from a life that doesn't. We would be able to say less,
'Here's what I want' and more 'What do you suppose God
wants?' We'd see our suffering differently. 'My pain
proves God's absence' would be replaced with 'My pain
expands God's purpose.' " [91]

The God-centered life places God at the center and
gives us perspective as to our own importance. If an
idealist is to grasp faith they must first embrace humility.

---

[91] Lucado, Max. It's Not about Me. (2004) Integrity Publishers

113

The Surprising Destroyer of Faith

Despite what a wounded idealist may think:

> Entitlement and *not* disappointment
> is the unexpected faith killer.

If you are put off by this notion, consider the case of the Canaanite woman recorded in Matthew. She was a Gentile with a demon-possessed daughter. (While some may think your children are possessed, her daughter was literally possessed by an evil spirit.) She may have been a widow or married to a non-believer, who disdained this Jewish preacher. Either way, she approached Jesus alone. She had no doubt faced her share of loss, disappointment, and rejection. And yet no example captures this humility-faith link quite like her interaction with Jesus does.

"Leaving that place, Jesus withdrew to the region of Tyre and Sidon. A Canaanite woman from that vicinity came to him, crying out, 'Lord, Son of David, have mercy on me! My daughter is demon-possessed and suffering terribly.' Jesus did not answer a word. So his disciples came to him and urged him, 'Send her away, for she keeps crying out after us'. He answered, 'I was sent only to the lost sheep of Israel.' The woman came and knelt before him. 'Lord, help me!' she said. He replied, 'It is not right to take the children's bread and toss it to the dogs.' 'Yes it is, Lord,' she said. 'Even the dogs eat the crumbs that fall from their master's table.' Then Jesus said to her, 'Woman, you have great faith! Your request is granted.' And her daughter was healed at that moment." [92]

Jesus withdrew to the region of Tyre and Sidon. It was the first time in his adult life that he left Israel. In modern times he would have needed a visa. It is here he meets the Canaanite woman. She had no doubt heard of Jesus and what he had been doing in Israel. She follows him crying out to him, but Jesus pays no attention to her. He ignores her. He acts like he doesn't see or hear a thing. Put yourself in her shoes. You come to Jesus with a desperate need, and this is the response you get. How would you be feeling and what would you do next?

The Canaanite woman had three obstacles to her faith.

- The first obstacle was: **God doesn't care about me.** If she had been an idealist, she would have immediately been put off by Jesus' lack of attention. "How can a loving God treat me this

---

[92] Matthew 15:21-28

115

way. I am not asking for something evil, or even really for myself." Idealists don't take kindly to being ignored or uncared about. But this woman was not an idealist. She faced the facts of her situation with faith. She had taken a chance asking Jesus to heal a non-Jew. Maybe she had counted the cost that he might not respond the first or second or third time. Rather than be offended she persevered. Her humility and need enabled her to do that.

So she perseveres to the point where the disciples get irritated with her and ask Jesus to send her away. Jesus responds by saying, "I was sent only to the lost sheep of Israel."

- The second obstacle to her faith was: **Maybe what I am asking for is not in the will of God.** If she had been an idealist, she might have been disappointed by Jesus' response and given up. The truth was that she was living outside the borders of Israel. She was not a Jew. (We know later Paul would preach to the Gentiles but *for now,* the Gentiles were NOT a part of God's will.) She understood the social barriers between Jews and Gentiles, but it did not deter her. It didn't move her. She just kept persevering. Her humility and her need enabled her to do that.

Finally, she gets down on her knees begging, "Lord, help me." Jesus responds, "It is not right to take the children's bread and toss it to the dogs." No, he didn't. Jesus Christ, the Lamb of God, meek and mild did not just say that!

Scholars say that this was a common phrase that Jews used. It's like the Texans say "everything is bigger and better in Texas." It is a phrase that is thrown around but not necessarily true. Jesus was testing her faith with this statement. In fact, the whole encounter was a test.

- The final obstacle her faith needed to overcome was: **Being racially offended.** How would you have responded to Jesus' comment?
  We can think of a few of our own reactions; anger, bitterness, and hurt. Thinking "if this is the kind of God you are, then I want nothing to do with you," or maybe "I deserve better treatment than this." "This is not fair. I have humbled myself, I have kept crying out, but enough is enough! It's time for God to do his part or I am out of here."

How different are those responses to this humble, faithful woman? She did not feel entitled, or that she deserved anything from God. Although she may not have understood everything that was happening, she was banking on God's character. Despite how things appeared, she trusted in his love and mercy, and this trust and humility enabled her daughter to be healed.

David R Hawkin's words ring true when he stated that:

A humble person cannot be humiliated.[93]

This woman was not humiliated by her encounter with Jesus. Quite the opposite! She was blessed by it. Her faith, enabled by her humility made that possible.

How About Us?

We will find faith in a place where God is the only option and all other options including our own pride and ego are removed. To answer the earlier question: "How does an idealist transition to faithful realism whilst circumventing the enticing lure of cynicism when disappointed?" The answer is humility.

---

[93] David R. Hawkins. Letting Go: The Pathway of Surrender. (2012). Hay House

To practice humility means to value other people and their opinions without indulging in self-pride.

Humility is the bridge an idealist must use to cross over the stormy waters of cynicism towards faith.

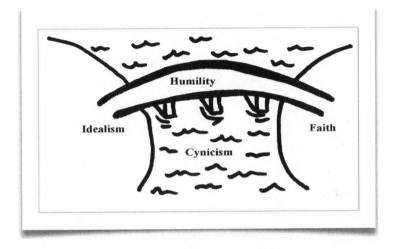

Life is going to disappoint us, people are going to let us down, it is inevitable. But humility provides a way out. It opens doors, opportunities, and healing that our egos won't allow. Humility is the birthplace of faith.

What Does This Faith Look Like?

Being an idealist comes with tremendous strengths. Idealists have vision, passion, zeal, and hope. They dream of making the world a better place. These qualities must not be smothered, if anything they need to be fanned into flame, but it can't stop there. Like all temperaments, idealists also have debilitating weaknesses. In order to avoid potential cynicism when disappointed, and to develop true faith, an idealist must apply humility to their weaknesses.

If we combine the tables from chapters three and six, and apply humility it would look something like this:

Weaknesses of Idealism		Faith
Self-sufficient	H	Asks for help or advice
Impractical	U	Listens without dismissing those who are more practical
Critical of others	M	Recognize own strengths and weaknesses without becoming boastful or self-deprecating
Rash, relies on emotions in decision-making	I	Take the time to weigh up all options and consider the effects of choices on self and others
Brave talker and dreamer Can be lazy	L	Willing to work hard and not rely on personality or charm to make up for a lack of diligence

Impatient Want to give up when it gets tough	I	Perseveres and humbles oneself before God when things don't work out, rather than to quit
Sets hope on a specific outcome Entitled before God	T	Trusts that God knows better than you and that your plans, as visionary as they may be, might not be best. There may be a better way
Unrealistic expectations of self and others	Y	Does not take failure so seriously or personally. Willing to take a risk and fail and get back up.

Humility in Action

Consider how this plays out in the following scenarios.

- Jolanda went to see a doctor complaining of a stomach ache. Within two weeks she was diagnosed with stage four intestinal cancer. Everyone around her told her to be positive and believe that God would work a miracle. As desperately as she wanted a miraculous healing, in humility she surrendered her life before God and prayed the prayer of Shadrach, Meshach, and Abednego:

"If we are thrown into the blazing furnace, the God we serve is able to deliver us from it, and he will

121

deliver us from Your Majesty's hand. But <u>even if</u>
<u>he does not</u>, we want you to know, Your Majesty,
that we will not serve your gods or worship the
image of gold you have set up. " [94]

She knew that God was able to heal her but determined
that even if he chose not to, she would still follow him.

- Juan wanted to buy an apartment. He viewed
  one that he loved instantly but was above his
  price range. He had made spontaneous
  purchases in the past that had landed him in
  trouble. Being an idealist, he was sure that this
  time he could make it work, if he cut his budget
  here and there. He remembered that faith, and
  not wishful thinking, was enabled by humility,
  so he decided to ask for some advice. When he
  crunched the numbers he realized he couldn't
  afford it. As disappointing as it was, he had
  actually been spared a lot of heartache.

- Patrick was so excited to get married. He had
  been living as a single Christian since he was
  15. He had dreamed about his wedding day.
  When the day finally arrived he was excited for

---

[94] Daniel 3:16-18 (emphasis added)

the anticipated honeymoon. Unfortunately, it didn't turn out how he had hoped. He felt embarrassed and ashamed at what he perceived as a failure. He applied humility to his wounded idealism and found the faith to get open with trusted friends and get the help he and his new bride needed.

- Sally joined the church because she loved the way the minister spoke. He had an ability to put into words what she felt in her heart. She felt inspired and convicted by his call to radical living. When the minister was exposed for living a double life, she was devastated. She considered throwing in the towel. She just wanted to give up. In humility she recognized that she had set her hope on a person and not on God. She decided to stay and fight for her faith and for God's church.

What a difference humility makes! It is the unsung hero to faith formation and emotional renewal.

Jesus said: "Come to me, all you who are weary and burdened, and I will give you rest. Take my yoke upon you and learn from me, for I am gentle and humble in heart, and you will <u>find</u> <u>rest</u> for your souls." [95]

Jesus changed the world for all eternity. He was a visionary leader and a brave preacher. He faced stiff opposition and constant criticism. He was able to see the reality of the sinful world around him yet was not discouraged by it. He was compassionate but not naïve. Bold and unashamed. But above all, *he was humble*. The true faithful realist.

May we have the humility to come to him and find rest for our souls; to learn from him and find healing for our wounds. And may we all be counted among the fellowship of the faithful. God bless.

---

[95] Matthew 11: 28 (emphasis added)

Resources

Appendix A: Advice for Ministers

If I cannot do great things,
I can do small things in a great way.
Martin Luther King, JR.

Idealism in The Church

The idealist and the church, could there ever be a better pairing? Well yes, that would be the idealist and heaven.

According to the Myers-Briggs personality type indicator:

"Idealists long for meaningful communication and relationships. Focused on the future, they are enthusiastic about possibilities, and they strive for self-renewal and personal growth. Idealists strive to discover who they are and how they can become their best possible self — always this quest for self-knowledge and self-improvement drives their imagination - and idealists yearn to help others make the journey too."[96]

---

[96] MyersBriggs/ExamplesOfIdealistPersonalitiesInStories

The church and her visionary purpose capture the imagination of idealistic leaders. They want to grow and help others to grow. [97] The mission to reach a lost world rouses a dream that is refreshingly bigger than them.

The church and her promise of relational connection capture the imagination of idealistic members. The promise of a transformed life and purpose stirs their souls. Idealistic leaders cast an idealistic vision, and idealistic followers eat it up. They express this vision with great passion and hyperbole. It's what resonates with idealists who want to hear how they are going to change the world and eliminate global poverty, and in their lifetime. The fact that Jesus says in Matthew "the poor you will always have with you," [98] is of little consequence to the idealist.

There is no place greater on earth than the church. Timothy describes it as, "God's household, the pillar and foundation of the truth."[99] But for an idealist, it doesn't end there. Yes, they bring into the church the desire for

---

[97] A litmus test for a true idealist is how eager they are to tell others about a discovery they have made. It doesn't even matter what it is; a book, a restaurant, a doctor with some specialty, or a wonder-working multi-vitamin. They cannot help but share. To not would be a disservice to their fellow man. A lack of enthusiasm from the recipient of the good news does not easily dissuade them.

[98] Matthew 26:11

[99] 1 Timothy 3:15

connection, growth, and purpose but they also bring expectations that a flawed people will never be able to live up to. They can set their hope on people or a mission statement instead of on God, and they can expect leaders to be perfect. Idealistic leaders can expect ministry results to come quickly and painlessly.

But what happens when everything is less than ideal? When it doesn't work as imagined, people get wounded. Leaders become disillusioned and apathetic. Members can become bitter and cynical. My leaders become *the leadership*. My church becomes *the* church.

So who's to blame, the leaders or the members? Well, both. Firstly, we need to be careful when giving a vision, and secondly, we need to be careful how we receive it. We have to have a balanced biblical view.

The church is the body of Christ; unfortunately, while it is still on earth, it is filled with sinners. Will people disappoint us? Absolutely! If that were not the case, Jesus would not have told his disciples that if your brother sins against you forgive him seven times 77 times. We are meant to bear with each other, cover over our grievances, and show mercy. Idealists get so surprised by conflict or problems in the church. Honestly, if we took Jesus at his word, we would not be surprised at all.

Looking Back To Move Forward

The first century church was incredible. It started in Jerusalem and by the end of the New Testament; it had reached to the corners of the Roman Empire. But it was not without its problems. Leaders weren't perfect; people resorted back to legalism and Jewish ideology. Sin crept into the church and factions formed. False teachers in Ephesus were causing all kinds of problems. The Corinthian church more closely resembled the world than the Kingdom of God, with people getting drunk at communion, a father and son in a relationship with the same woman and factions forming based on influential personalities. The Galatian churches were returning to Judaism with circumcision and Jewish dietary laws being re-implemented. By the end of the book of Acts, we have some great churches and some very messy churches!

Sometimes, those of us who have been around awhile are concerned about what happened to the Acts 2 church we are trying to build. While we should always strive to imitate the church in Acts 2, we must remember that 30 years on, even the churches built by the apostles, had their problems. Some were strong; some were weak. They had their strong Smyrna and Philadelphia, their flawed

Thyatira, Ephesus, and Pergamum, their lukewarm Laodicea and their dead Sardis.

We are no longer a young church, and like the first-century group, we have our similar strong, medium and weak churches. The answer is not to desert the disciples and start something new, as some have done. We will just end up right where the apostles did in Asia, with a collection of strong, medium and weak churches. No! The answer is to make a decision to continue the fight for our generation. At the end of the book of Acts, with a lifetime of ministry behind him, Paul "Boldly and without hindrance, preached the Kingdom of God and taught about the Lord Jesus Christ."[100] Paul maintained his faith till the end and avoided becoming cynical.

So as ministers and leaders, how can we better equip the next generation of young idealists?

Although we can't prevent young idealists from being wounded later in life, we can certainly provide them with tools to help them overcome. Successful youth ministries which produce men and women of lasting convictions, are those infused with faith and inspiration *as well as* balanced deeper teaching about the reality of life. Idealistic youth

---

[100] Acts 28:30-31

ministers must be careful how they present the gospel to young, impressionable minds.

For example, one time our daughter came back from a "fired-up" youth event feeling very discouraged. We were surprised and asked what had been preached. She told us that the zealous youth leader had spoken about changing the world and having global impact. When asked why that would discourage her, she replied, "how am I going to change the world when I can't even get a friend to come to church with me?" The hype and expectation had overwhelmed and deflated her. While we were sure that many were inspired by the message, it had actually produced the exact opposite effect on our daughter.

It's easy for youth leaders to feel that they always have to have high-energy "cheer sessions" when standing in front of teens and campus students; and while the youth do need that inspiration, it must be balanced. Ministers must help the youth understand that while they may not change the world tomorrow, they can help to change other people's lives, one person at a time, starting with themselves!

Helpful Topics for an Idealist to Study in the Bible

(These are also great topics to expand on and include in your teaching schedule.)

- **Fear of God and Humility**

In the council of the holy ones God is greatly feared;
he is more awesome than all who surround him.

Psalm 89:7

This is one of the most fundamental concepts for a young idealist to grasp. They will not be humble in their interactions with others if they do not understand humility and surrender before God. Before they dream big, they need to understand their place before God. They need to have respect for who they are dealing with. One idea is to study out the Book of Job, not all of it, but chapters 1-2 with some historical context. Then get the young idealists to write out their own version of Job 38-39. i.e. all the things about this world and creation that they can't comprehend.

- **Mercy**

Mercy triumphs over judgment. James 2:13

Young idealists can be pretty judgmental. They enjoy giving their opinions even at the cost of offending others. Help them to learn what matters to God. Being merciful and seeing the good is more noble in God's eyes than noticing everything that is wrong.

- **Patience and Impatience, Contentment and Discontent**

Better a patient person than a warrior, one with self-control than one who takes a city. Proverbs 16:32

Patience, patience, patience, patience. How do you get five years of ministry experience (or work or life experience)? By being in the ministry five years. Character development takes time. Help these young people.

- **Perseverance and Endurance**

Not only so, but we also glory in our sufferings, because we know that suffering produces perseverance; perseverance, character; and character, hope. Romans 5:3-4

135

Unlike good looks, athletic ability or musical talent, which are given at birth, strength of character is forged in the fire of life. Teach them to grow in the areas that don't come easily or naturally to them and not to just focus on their obvious gifts.

- **Hard work and Laziness, Faith and Deeds**

Those who work their land will have abundant food, but those who chase fantasies have no sense.
Proverbs 12:11

Help them to be successful by giving them the ideas, plans and tools necessary to accomplish their dreams. They really have no clue how hard they have to work.

- **Suffering**

Consider it pure joy, my brothers and sisters, whenever you face trials of many kinds. James 1:2

Jesus spoke about suffering a lot. He didn't shy away from the subject or try to candy-coat it. As a youth minister, don't always rescue or feel sorry for the kids you minister to every time they go through a hard time. While showing empathy, help them to find God in the hardship. Psalm 107 is a phenomenal passage to study out with idealists who struggle with suffering in the world as a whole.

We must help young men and women to have the strength of character to face the temptations that Satan will throw at them. Let us diligently work with God's Spirit to prepare them.

Appendix B: Changing your view of God

The purpose of this worksheet is to help change a distorted view of God. Satan wants to get us to doubt God, lose trust in his love and ultimately walk away from him. He has used a distorted view of God to sabotage faith since the Garden of Eden and his tactics are no different today. If we are going to overcome, we must be able to recognize his schemes. In a prediction made about the destruction of Jerusalem, Daniel tells of how with "flattery, he [Satan] will corrupt those who have violated the covenant, but the people **who know their God** will firmly resist him."[101] It would be the Israelites who knew their God who would resist Satan's deception. They would resist not because they were Israelites or attended synagogue and obligatory prayers. No, they would resist because they knew God.

As Christians, we are not immune to Satan's disingenuous allure. We will face our own ups and downs, with Satan right there, whispering lies into our ears. As with the Israelites, the Christians who will be able to stand

---

[101] Daniel 11:32 (emphasis added)

till the end will be the ones who *know their God.* A legalistic duty to fulfill the requirements of the faith will not enable us to withstand Satan's attacks.

Our knowledge of God is the starting point for godly living. It affects every area of our lives. In 1 Thessalonians, Paul attributes the source of impurity and heathen behavior to not knowing God.

It is God's will that you should be sanctified: that you should avoid sexual immorality; that each of you should learn to control his own body in a way that is holy and honorable, not in passionate lust like the heathen, **who do not know God.** [102]

When we know God and his true nature, he inspires us to live self-controlled, holy lives. In the Garden of Gethsemane Jesus prayed for us to know God.

Now THIS is eternal life: that **they may know you,** the only true God[103]

Knowing God is eternal life. It is the crux of Christianity, yet so often we miss the point. It's not

---

[102] 1 Thessalonians 4: 3–5 (emphasis added)
[103] John 17:3 (emphasis added)

enough to know the right things to do or say, we must know God.

In 2 Peter 1:2-3, Peter tells us that as we grow in our knowledge of God, grace and peace can be ours in abundance. He goes on to say that we will have everything we need for life and godliness through this same knowledge. When we face difficulties in life, God should be the safe place we run to, not from. He must be for us a haven where we find comfort, courage and perspective, not judgment and condemnation. We must grow in the knowledge of God. For us to do this, we must first identify our misconceptions about God.

Step one: Knowing who *God is Not*

> We demolish arguments and every pretension
> that sets itself up **against the knowledge of**
> **God**, and we take captive every thought to make
> it obedient to Christ.[104]

The Bible teaches us to demolish every lie or pretension that sets itself up against the knowledge of God. We must capture them at thought level. Many of these lies were put into our minds at an early age, while we were still impressionable. It is our responsibility now, as adults, to

---

[104] 2 Corinthians 10:5 (emphasis added)

identify them and challenge them with the truth of who God is.

God our Father

One of the easiest ways that Satan distorts our view of God is by using the image of God as a father *against* us.

Depending on your relationship with your earthly father, the notion of God the Father may bring comfort and reassurance. But to others, the "father image" can be daunting and unpredictable. Without being aware of what we are thinking, we can project the image of our physical fathers onto our view of God. We then interpret what happens in our lives based on this faulty view, affirming our already warped view of God. God *is* our father but He *is not* a reflection of our earthly fathers. He is the perfect father, our heavenly Father.

To help us identify the faulty images we project onto God, let us look at a few examples of how our interactions with our physical fathers can affect our view of God.

Absent fathers – This father was absent from birth. Either he left the family or passed away when the child was too young to know him. It may be that the child has no idea who the father is.

Possible spiritual repercussion: As thankful as you may be for God wanting to be your father, you may have learned out of necessity to be self-reliant and live independently. Satan wants you to believe that you don't have a deep need for God. He tries to kill any desire to be close to God. Consequently, sin becomes a matter of right and wrong with little heart connection. You can feel a sense that God is distant and unconcerned about your daily challenges. Bible study and prayer can become academic and duty bound.

Present but absent fathers – This father was not a good communicator. He was unable to express his feelings, or say "I love you". He was almost an observer and not involved with the family.

Possible spiritual repercussion: With a father who does not meet emotional needs, a child feels fragile, starved emotionally and not confident they can have a close relationship with God. You may not trust God's love or else find it difficult to bond with God emotionally. You may feel it is your fault that your father could not love you, leaving you feeling guilty, unlovable and fearful. Often there are feelings of shame for needing to be loved. Trying to fill the gap left by an emotionally detached father, you can tend to be dependent on other people or other "things" for emotional security. An uninvolved father also does not help a person know how to establish good boundaries, which has many spiritual implications.

Alcoholic – Weekend (functional) or full-time. For children growing up in the home of an alcoholic, life can become a series of lies and pretense. Some children live with a lot of embarrassment about their fathers and therefore they survive by learning to pretend "everything is fine." Pretension is putting up a false front to gain acceptance.

<u>Possible spiritual repercussion</u>: It is easy to be fake, and superficial. It can be frightening and difficult to be honest with others about how you are doing spiritually. Having an unstable alcoholic father has a profound effect in many areas of building a trusting close relationship with God and others. Openness with a spiritual friend is essential to help you figure out all the ways Satan distorts your view of God.

Authoritarian/Harsh Disciplinarian - With this type of father nothing is ever good enough. His harsh motivation leaves a child feeling guilty and inept.

Possible spiritual repercussion: An authoritarian father can make you believe that you are always a disappointment to God. Without help to develop a healthy internal motivation, you may constantly need rewards or praise to feel good about yourself or be motivated. In a family with two or more children, the siblings may feel the need to compete. Because of this father figure influencing our image of God, you may become overly concerned with your performance and place in the church. Satan can also use this image to get you to believe that it is hopeless to attain God's perfect standard so you should give up trying.

Insecure Fathers - This type of father finds it difficult to deal with failure or perceived failure in himself or his children. He may be too fearful to set up rules and boundaries that are good for the child out of fear of losing the child's favor. Or he may act out his insecurity through frequent bouts of anger and control. Again, a child will imitate his insecurity, or disrespect him for it. The inconsistency is confusing.

Possible spiritual repercussion: It is difficult for you to maintain faith in the consistency of God. You look for meaning or signs in life events. You can misinterpret them as God being angry with you or that you have been able to manipulate God to get your way.

Physically or verbally abusive fathers – Just as in all unhealthy relationships, what we hope for is love but what we get is pain. Because of being raised by an abusive parent a child will learn to avoid or soothe their pain in their own way. A child may respond in anger, resentment and rebellion outwardly or inwardly. The bottom line is survival.

Possible spiritual repercussion: You may feel like, "I will not let God dominate me," or you may be motivated to do the right thing out of a fear of being punished. Healthy discipline and conflict resolution are foreign concepts to be feared or avoided. Again, the purpose of Satan's lie is to leave us distant and afraid of God.

Fathers who showed unconditional love and support While this should seem like a great image to project onto God, even with this image, Satan corrupts. It is much easier to see and accept God's unconditional love with this father image, but you can still be deceived spiritually by losing your awe and appreciation of God.

Possible spiritual repercussion: The challenge remains for you to take personal responsibility to be honest, consistent and disciplined in being and staying close to God. It's easy to rely on the knowledge of being

145

loved and not on consistent daily devotion to prayer and Bible study. Satan wants you to take your relationship with God for granted and so let your guard down.

Hen-pecked fathers – Mom ruled the house and she was the dominating influence in your life. Women tend to be a lot pickier than men and a lot more critical of others. You may have seen this in your home and feared coming under the same judgments. Raised in this environment can leave you feeling second best. Mom's critical eye, even of their father, can leave a child feeling the need to measure up.

Possible spiritual repercussion: You can feel a need to perform for God to win His "approval". It can be difficult to feel that you can be loved unconditionally for just being you when living under constant judgment of what you say and do. The hen-pecked father will not call his wife to treat the children righteously. With this father image influencing us we may doubt God's loyalty and ability to protect us.

These are just some examples of how our relationship with our physical fathers can affect the way we see God. You may be able to relate to one or more of them. We each have our own experiences.

The goal in going through this is for us to become self-aware in identifying Satan's lies. If we are aware that Satan's plan is to destroy our relationship with God, we can challenge our false beliefs.

We can break their hold on us by surrendering them to the truth about God in the Bible. Without this awareness, Satan can use our emotions and experiences as faulty, untrustworthy guides.

Step two: The Truth of Who God Is

> And so we know and rely on the love God has for us. God is love.[105]

The bible teaches that God is love. Love defines God and God defines love. But perhaps the word love is vague and confusing to us. Let's break it down.

God is Love

If God is love, then 1Corinthians 13:4-8 gives us an in-depth description of who God is. This *is the truth* about God.

God is patient,

---

[105] 1 John 4:16

God is kind,
God is not proud,
God is not rude,
God is not self-seeking, or insist on its own way.
God is not easily angered, or irritable or resentful.
God does not envy,
God does not boast,
God does not keep a record of wrongs.
God does not delight in evil but rejoices with the truth.
God always protects,
God always trusts,
God always hopes,
God always perseveres.
God never fails!

Take a deep breath and meditate on these thoughts. Our encouragement is that you can take the next couple of weeks to study out God's character as described from 1 Corinthians 13.

Here's How

- Take a characteristic a day and apply it to your life i.e. God is patient with _____ (put your name there)
- Now write down whether you believe that statement to be true and why or why not.

- Write down specific situations in your life that make you believe that "truth" or non-truth.
- Next, find 5 or 6 other verses that talk about God's patience with you.
- The next day (or days) repeat this exercise with "God is Kind" with _____.
- Keep going until you have worked through each characteristic.

This exercise can take you days, weeks or months.

We encourage you to take the time to build a solid foundation in your relationship with God. If you've been a Christian for a long time, then this is an excellent opportunity to fill in the gaps in the foundation you already have. If you are new in your relationship with God, take time to build a strong foundation on the truth.

When the treasury trains people to identify forged dollar bills they don't do it by showing them all the fake bills ever printed. Instead they train them so thoroughly about what a real bill looks like, that it becomes *easy to spot a fake.* Our prayer is that as you intently study out the nature of God, it will become easy for you to spot Satan's lies so that you can live victoriously in the knowledge of God.

To contact the authors please visit

www.goodreads.com/author/show/17007645.Justin_and_Irene_Renton

Or visit our Facebook page

www.facebook.com/Healing-of-a-Wounded-Idealist-159021571304086

Made in the USA
San Bernardino, CA
28 June 2020

74343303R00093